THE HOUSE ARREST OF ZHANG XUELIANG

THE HOUSE ARREST
of
ZHANG
XUELIANG

◇◇◇

A Memoir of Growing Up with China's
Most Famous Political Prisoner

Bernard Liu

CARUACHI LLC
Virginia Beach

ISBN Paperback: 979-8-9855679-0-8
ISBN eBook: 979-8-9855679-1-5

Library of Congress Control Number: 2022900197

Edited by Sylvia Liu
Proofread by Louise Stahl
Chinese and pinyin copyedits by Yilin Wang
Cover design by Robin Locke Monda
Interior design by Glen M. Edelstein

Caruachi LLC
3419 Virginia Beach Blvd #405
Virginia Beach, VA 23452

Publisher's Cataloging-in-Publication data

Names: Liu, Bernard, author.
Title: The house arrest of Zhang Xueliang : a memoir of growing up with China's most famous political prisoner / Bernard Liu.
Description: Includes bibliographical references. | Virginia Beach, VA: Caruachi LLC, 2022.
Identifiers: LCCN: 2022900197 | ISBN: 979-8-9855679-0-8 (paperback) | 979-8-9855679-1-5 (ebook)
Subjects: LCSH Liu, Bernard. | Zhang, Xueliang, 1901-2001---Captivity. | Generals--China--Anecdotes. | China--History--1937-. | China--History--20th century. | BISAC BIOGRAPHY & AUTOBIOGRAPHY / Personal Memoirs | HISTORY / Asia / China | HISTORY / Military / Wars & Conflicts | HISTORY / Wars & Conflicts / World War II / Pacific Theater | POLITICAL SCIENCE / World / Asian | POLITICAL SCIENCE / Political Ideologies / Communism, Post-Communism & Socialism
Classification: LCC DS777.488.C465 .L58 2022 | DDC 951.04/2/0924--dc23

To my father, mother,
sister, brothers, my wife Terry,
and my daughters Vivian and Sylvia

THE HOUSE ARREST OF ZHANG XUELIANG

INTRODUCTION

This is my story about growing up with the famous Chinese political figure, Zhang Xueliang (張學良), who lived with my father, Liu Yiguang (劉乙光), for twenty-five years of Zhang's house arrest.

In 1936, General Zhang Xueliang instigated the Xi'an Incident and changed the course of Chinese history. As a result, he was placed under house arrest by the Guomindang (國民黨), the Nationalist Party that ruled China before 1949. The house arrest lasted for fifty years. My father, Liu Yiguang, who worked for the military intelligence agency, was charged with the day-to-day supervision and control of Zhang Xueliang for the first twenty-five years of that house arrest, from 1936 to 1962.

Zhang Xueliang was one of Generalissimo Chiang Kai-shek's generals who changed the course of Chinese history in the Xi'an Incident of 1936. The Communists were about to be decimated by the Nationalists during their civil war, when General Zhang Xueliang ignored Chiang Kai-shek's direct orders to eliminate the Communists. Instead, he kidnapped Chiang Kai-shek and forced him to agree to stop fighting the Communists and to focus on the Japanese threat. This allowed the Communists to recover their strength and eventually defeat the Nationalists years later and take control of China in 1949. Zhang Xueliang is considered a national hero today by China for saving the Communist Party from defeat at its weakest time.

After the Xi'an Incident, upon release, Chiang Kai-shek arrested his former general and placed him under house arrest. My father, Liu Yiguang, military commander in the Guomindang Intelligence Agency, was charged with overseeing the house arrest of Mr. Zhang. For the next ten years in the Mainland and fifteen years in Taiwan, from 1936 to 1962, Zhang Xueliang lived in the Liu family compound, moving twelve times over the years (ten times in mainland China to avoid Japanese attacks during World War II).

My mother, my siblings, and I lived nearby or in the compounds themselves. I lived with them during summer and winter vacations. We ate meals with Mr. Zhang and his mistress, heard his stories, and witnessed twenty-five years of his life that were largely unknown to the general public.

This is the untold story of the twenty-five years Zhang Xueliang was under house arrest, based on my and my family's memories. Any mistakes in the telling are my own.

Chapter One

HISTORICAL BACKGROUND

I'm not a historian, but I will provide some historical background about Zhang Xueliang and his influence on Chinese history.[1]

MODERN CHINA'S TUMULTUOUS START

The period of Chinese history from the establishment of the Republic of China in 1912 (under Nationalist Party rule) to the People's Republic of China in 1949 (under Communist Party rule), was a complex and difficult time. In that period, China struggled to unify after the fall of the Qing Dynasty and the rise of warlords, endured a civil war between the Nationalists and the Communists, and fought against Japanese invasion in the Second Sino-Japanese War (part of the Pacific Theater of World War II).

When the Qing Dynasty fell in 1912, Sun Yat-sen founded

---

1. My daughter and editor Sylvia Liu helped write the overview leading up to the Xi'an Incident.

the Republic of China under the rule of the Nationalist Party, the Guomindang. He soon lost power, and the Warlord Period (1916-1928) ensued, where warlords fought for control, and Japan sought to increase its influence in northern China. In the early 1920s, Sun Yat-sen regained power in the south. The Communist Party was founded in 1921, and the Communists dominated the left-wing of the Guomindang. In 1925, Sun Yat-sen's successor, right-leaning Chiang Kai-shek (蔣介石), took over and purged the Communists from the Guomindang in 1927. In 1928, Chiang Kai-shek led a military campaign (the Northern Expedition) to unify the country, successfully capturing Beijing.

Zhang Xueliang (張學良) was the eldest son of Zhang Zuolin (張作霖), the warlord of Manchuria from 1916 to 1928 who controlled 960,000 square kilometers of land. By 1924, Zhang Zuolin had moved south into China itself, controlling Beijing. As Chiang Kai-shek's army approached Beijing in 1928, Zhang Zuolin retreated, and on June 4, 1928, was assassinated by the Japanese. At the age of twenty-seven, Zhang Xueliang inherited his father's mantle as leader of Northeast China.

On December 27, 1928, Zhang Xueliang declared allegiance to the Guomindang and Chiang Kai-shek, which resulted in Chiang unifying China and becoming the country's highest leader, the Generalissimo. Zhang Xueliang was promoted to a three-star general and became the secondhand man of Chiang Kai-shek. Zhang Xueliang was known as the Young Marshal (少帥). At the time, Zhang Xueliang was a playboy and an opium addict, but he proved to be a capable and savvy leader, introducing modernizing reforms to Manchuria.

Figure 1 Zhang Xueliang as a young man

Figure 2 l to r: Zhang Xueliang, Chiang Kai-shek

On September 18, 1931, Japanese troops attacked the military headquarters of the Northeast at Shenyang. Zhang Xueliang and Chiang Kai-shek were not ready to fight the Japanese yet. Zhang Xueliang decided not to resist and withdrew 200,000 Northeastern troops to the south of the Great Wall, resulting in the loss of the entire Northeast (Manchuria) to Japan. Japan set up the puppet state of Manchukuo, and the Japanese occupation would last until the Soviet Union invaded Manchuria in 1945.

Between 1927 and 1937, the Communist Party launched an insurgency against the Nationalist government, resulting in a ten-year civil war between the Red Army led by Mao Zedong (毛澤東) and the Nationalist government led by Chiang Kai-shek.

THE XI'AN INCIDENT

In 1936, Chiang Kai-shek ordered General Zhang Xueliang to lead his 200,000-strong Northeast army to eliminate the Communists. Chiang Kai-shek believed the Communists were a graver threat to the country than the Japanese. By the end of the year, the Communist Party's top leaders, Mao Zedong, Zhou Enlai (周恩來), and 25,000 troops were surrounded by Zhang Xueliang in Yan'an. Chiang Kai-shek came to Xi'an to supervise and ordered Zhang Xueliang to wipe out the Communist Party. However, Zhang Xueliang identified with communism and did not want to kill his fellow Chinese. He wanted to fight the Japanese.

On December 12, 1936, General Zhang Xueliang and General Yang Hucheng kidnapped Chiang Kai-shek and imprisoned him for thirteen days, until Chiang Kai-shek agreed to end the civil war with the Communists and fight the Japanese instead. Zhang Xueliang was pivotal in brokering the unofficial agreement between Chiang Kai-shek and Communist Party delegate Zhou Enlai to end the civil war. This became known as the Xi'an Incident, which saved the Communist Party from defeat during a period when they were most weak, and thereby, changed Chinese history.

As a result of the Xi'an Incident, the civil war was halted, allowing the Communists to build up considerable strength over the next ten years, as the Nationalists and Communists fought against the Japanese. When World War II ended, the Chinese civil war resumed from 1946 to 1949, resulting in millions of lives lost, and the establishment of the People's Republic of China.

ARREST OF ZHANG XUELIANG

On December 25, 1936, Zhang Xueliang accompanied Chiang Kai-shek back to Nanjing. He ordered one of his planes to take Chiang Kai-shek to Nanjing, and he took another one forty minutes later.

Chiang Kai-shek landed in Nanjing and received a very warm welcome.

When Zhang Xueliang landed in Nanjing, waiting for him was my father, Chief Special Agent (特務頭子)Liu Yiguang (劉乙光) and twenty special agents. They immediately arrested him and escorted him to a guest house.

After a trial before a military court, Zhang Xueliang was sentenced to ten years imprisonment, but Chiang Kai-shek pardoned him and placed him under house arrest for his role in the Xi'an Incident. He called it "Control" (管束). My father, Liu Yiguang, was delegated the day-to-day task of supervising Zhang Xueliang's house arrest.

ONE FAMILY

For the next twenty-five years, from 1936 to 1962, Zhang Xueliang lived under the same roof or in the same compound with my father in both mainland China and Taiwan, with our family nearby. I spent summer and winter vacations living with them. My family lived with them under the same roof during some of the Taiwan years.

What was Mr. Zhang's day-to-day life like during those twenty-five years? Aside from my siblings, I am one of the few people still alive with memories of that period (I was between the ages of four and twenty-nine when he was under my father's supervision). My sister Theresa took many of the photos in this memoir. My brother Philip's memories are included in the memoir, and my sister Theresa's and my brother Frank's recollections are included at the end of this account.

The photo was taken at Mr. Zhang's 60th birthday in 1961. In the first row, from left to right, are my mother Long Zhizu (龍志祖), Zhang Xueliang, Edith Chao (Zhao Yidi, 趙一荻, known to us as Miss Four[2]), and my father Liu Yiguang (劉乙光). In the second row, from left to right, are me, the author, Bernard Liu (Liu Shoutze, 劉叔慈, No. 3), Frank Liu (Liu Jisen, 劉季森, No. 5), Theresa Walker (Liu Guanchan, 劉貫蟾, No. 4 and the only girl in our

---

2 Zhang's mistress, Miss Four, lived with him for twenty years of his house arrest and thereafter. Mrs. Zhang lived with Zhang for the first five years of his house arrest until 1942. In 1964, Zhang divorced his wife and married Miss Four.

family), Liu Bohan (劉伯涵, No. 1), and Alex Liu (Liu Zhongbo, 劉重伯, No. 6). Philip Liu (Liu Zhongpu, 劉仲璞, No. 2), was not there, as he was studying in the United States at that time.

Figure 3 Liu Family with Zhang Xueliang and Zhao Yidi (1961)

Mr. Zhang liked to talk, and he talked loudly. Whenever we ate together, we had seven or eight dishes of rich food, mostly meat. He would finish eating first—he was the person who moved his mouth the fastest while eating that I've ever seen in my life—and would begin to talk.

Miss Four and my parents ate slowly and listened to him. My brothers and sister ate fast and listened. I ate very fast and listened—my stomach was more developed than my brain.

It was always a treat to eat with him because we were able to eat meat when we dined with him. At our own home, it was a different story. In the ten years in mainland China, when we ate on our own, we ate four or five bowls of rice with one dish (such as boiled pumpkin) to push the rice down. For the fifteen years we lived in Taiwan, we ate slightly better—we had four bowls of rice with two dishes, such as one fish and one vegetable, to do the job.

During those twenty-five years, Mr. Zhang never talked about the Xi'an Incident. He liked to talk about his father, the Manchurian warlord Zhang Zuolin, sharing his stories and legends. He also liked to talk about his own past before the Xi'an Incident, and he had a lot of good, as well as, dirty jokes.

Listening to him repeat his stories so many times over the twenty-five years, I could remember them by heart.

Zhang Xueliang's life after 1962 is no longer a secret. There are many published materials on the Internet and in other sources. When writing the Chinese version of my memoir (*House Arrest Days of Zhang Xueliang*, People's Publishing House, 2018), I reviewed some of the public information to give an overview of Mr. Zhang's story from 1962 to 2001 (when he was 62 to 100 years old). In this English-language version, I've added more historical background, family anecdotes and photographs, and words written by my sister Theresa Walker and my brother Frank Liu.

This memoir will give readers my story of Zhang Xueliang's years under house arrest.

Chapter Two

WALKING INTO THE TRAP HIMSELF

As the Xi'an Incident came to a close, on December 25, 1936, Zhang Xueliang sent one of his airplanes to take Chiang Kai-shek and Madame Chiang to Nanjing, where they received a celebrated welcome.

On December 26, Zhang Xueliang flew to Nanjing with his staff and about twenty guards. His C3 airplane had two rows of canvas seats facing each other, with an empty space in between. Zhang Xueliang filled the space with all his baggage. He carried these with him for the next twenty-five years he was under house arrest. Later, it was discovered that they included national treasures better than the collection in the Chinese National Museum.

When they landed at Nanjing airport, he was picked up by twenty-one special agents sent by the intelligence chief Dai Li (戴笠).[3]

---

3 Dai Li was a natural special agent genius. He didn't have a teacher; he figured out things by himself. But he ran a lot of special agent training classes.

My father Liu Yiguang was the leader of the team.

They sent Zhang Xueliang as a guest to the mansion of Song Ziwen (宋子文), premier of China and brother-in-law of Chiang Kai-shek.

At that time, only Special Agent Xiong Zhongqing (熊仲清) entered the gate, to watch from a distance. He had very sharp ears and heard Zhang Xueliang ask Song Ziwen when they were walking, "Will the chairman shoot me?"

Song said, "No! No!"

Instead, Zhang Xueliang was placed under house arrest after some legal formalities.

My father was assigned by Chief Dai Li to guard Zhang Xueliang. Twenty-five years later, he was relieved of the duty.

Xikou, Zhejiang:
January - November 1937

On January 13, 1937, my father led the special agents and took Zhang Xueliang to Xikou, Zhejiang (浙江溪口), the hometown of Chiang Kai-shek. This would be the first of many moves over the next ten years, as Chiang Kai-shek kept Zhang Xueliang close to him while waging war against the Japanese and later the Communists.

In Xikou, they stayed in China Travel Service, a government operated hotel. Mr. Zhang's wife, Yu Fengzhi (于鳳至), joined him, and she would remain with him until 1942. They took over the whole hotel for more than nine months.

When they left, they burned it down (accidentally).

My father took their chief cook, Master Chan (陳大師父) and a waiter, Ami (阿迷)(he was called 西崽阿迷, where 西崽 loosely meant "the waiter who knew how to serve Western food"). They stayed with us as the cook and waiter for Zhang Xueliang until the end of the War of Resistance against Japan in 1945.

Zhang Xueliang was sent to the military court for trial and was sentenced to ten years imprisonment. But Chiang Kai-shek pardoned him and instead put him under "strict control," which was the house arrest that resulted in the 37-year-old "Young Marshal" losing his freedom for the next fifty years and disappearing from public view.

Figure 4 Zhang Xueliang in Xikou (1937)

11

The chief of the Guomindang secret police Dai Li sent my father, Liu Yiguang, as the captain of the special agent team (who he promoted to colonel), to "control" Zhang Xueliang.

Dai Li's instructions to my father were:

> Protect Zhang Xueliang. Do not let him commit suicide, escape, or be kidnapped. Observe his words and actions and record and report to him in writing.

My father kept a diary every day as part of this mandate. He had to report on everything Zhang Xueliang did and said over the years. After he was no longer in charge of Mr. Zhang, my father destroyed his diaries. He decided he no longer had a duty to keep the diaries, and he didn't want other people to read them.

My father was to supply materials to Zhang Xueliang as abundantly as possible and maintain a respectful attitude.

Chiang Kai-shek's instruction was "嚴加防範,相對自由" which meant my dad was to take "strict precautions" against Zhang Xueliang but allow him to be "relatively free." How strict? How much freedom? That was a problem for my father to figure out.

At the height of his power, Dai Li supervised nearly 50,000 special agents at the headquarters of the Bureau of Investigation and Statistics, the Guomindang's military intelligence agency, in Nanjing. He controlled the traffic police corps of the metropolis and the railway, the guerrillas, the Loyalty Salvation Army, and the more than 40,000 pirates along the southeast coast. Altogether, some

200,000 people were under his command.

The government's funding for this task was far from sufficient. Dai Li collected money himself. A U.S. special agent chief said he was "self-financing."

His money was not under the control of the audit department of the government. Dai Li spent money generously. He was not stingy; he looked at the big picture. Dai Li was capable and loyal to Chiang Kai-shek. The Japanese and traitors were afraid of him.

The activists of the Communist Party were also restrained by him. Zhou Enlai said that if Dai Li hadn't died, the Mainland would have been liberated a few years later.

On March 17, 1945, Dai Li crashed in a plane and died. The onsite inspection concluded that the aircraft was blown up by a bomb in the airplane. When Dai Li died, all units under his single-line command were disconnected.

The mighty Military Statistics Bureau was changed to the Military Intelligence Bureau. The number of people and the functions were greatly reduced.

The former Lieutenant General Zhang Yifu (張毅夫), who was Dai Li's second in command, failed to become the director, and Dai Li's secretary Mao Renfeng (毛人鳳) took the post.

My father, Liu Yiguang, a native of Hunan, graduated from the fourth class of the Whampoa Military Academy (黃埔軍校).[4] He participated in the Northern Expedition and worked as a political instructor for the combat troops. Later, he joined Dai Li's spy organization.

---

4. The Whampoa Military Academy was founded by Sun Yat-sen in 1924 and supplied the leadership of China's military (both Communists and Guomindang) in the country's important conflicts in the first half of the 20th century (the Northern Expedition, the civil war, the Second Sino-Chinese War).

Figure 5 Li Yiguang (undated)

My father was among the first at the Hong Gong Temple (洪公祠) training class run by Dai Li, the first training class Dai Li organized. The trainees were selected from one or two potential mid-level officers from each division of the Northern Expedition. After one year of training, they were told that they were "special agents," and were asked whether they wanted to leave.

At that point, they could have left, or they could have stayed. If they chose to stay, they were not allowed to leave for life. As a result, no one left, and most of them were Dai Li's main cadres in the future.

My father became the captain of Chiang Kai-shek's guard. He later transferred to Dai Li's headquarters in Nanjing, as a lieutenant colonel in charge of internal discipline.

Chapter Three

PINGXIANG, JIANGXI:
November 24 - December 22, 1937

Pingxiang (萍鄉) is a small town in Jiangxi Province (江西). We were lucky to find a small two-story Western style house. A pair of retired professors from Qinghua University lived with their seventeen-year-old daughter. They volunteered to move downstairs and rent the other rooms to us. My father told the accountant to pay a high rental price. Mr. Zhang, Mrs. Zhang, and my father lived upstairs. The owner and the guests got along well. The girl often went to Mrs. Zhang's room to listen to the gramophone.

In Pingxiang, there was nothing to see, and the weather was bad. Mr. Zhang mostly read books at home. One time, Mr. Zhang and his agents visited a coal mine and came back shortly after because it was unsafe and not fun. Another time, they went to explore a long cave. Mr. Zhang told the agents to use torches only. The agents obeyed but hid some flashlights in their pockets. The torches were fun, but if they went out, they couldn't let Mr. Zhang walk in the dark. They walked for a long time and finally found some footprints of a small animal. It was getting interesting! But near the end of the cave, they saw some large animal's footprints. Without one word, everyone just turned around and hurried back. Some special agents!

❊ ❊ ❊

CHENZHOU, HUNAN:
DECEMBER 1937 - MARCH 1938

In December 1937, the Japanese army had entered Jiangxi. Dai Li sent a telegram and told us to move to Chenzhou, Hunan Province (湖南郴州). At that time, the "borrowed" cars were sufficient, and more than a dozen drivers who were originally civilians had essentially become special agents. The fleet traveled as usual, "borrowing" gasoline and arriving at Qifengdu (棲鳳渡) near Chenzhou.

There was a large compound where they could stay for a short time. Deputy Xu went ahead with a few agents to Chenzhou to find a suitable compound to live in. He found a Taoist temple, Suxianguan (蘇仙觀), at Suxianling (蘇仙嶺), five miles from the county capital. There were more than one hundred rooms where Taoist priests lived.

It was seven miles from the foot of the hill to the gate of the temple. There were many stone steps along the way, both sides lined with large pine trees. As my father walked from the foot of the hill to the temple, he felt very spiritual.

Unfortunately, reality came crashing down. After returning, he told Deputy Xu to take some agents and give them a large amount of money to give to the hundreds of

Taoist priests to rent their own places somewhere else. Suxianguan had been rented to us.

Craftsmen were asked to renovate a few rooms for the Zhangs. Mr. Zhang liked to take a shower every day, so they deliberately made a large tub in the house. Many cauldrons in the kitchen could heat water, and there was good spring water on the mountain. The bearers carried it miles uphill every day to the kitchen.

All the other people, even the military police, lived in the temple.

The atmosphere was inspiring. My father began to read about and later began to believe in the Buddha (even though they lived in a Taoist temple).

The bearers went to Chengzhou to buy food every day, but there was no fruit in that town. They had to go to Changsha, many miles away, to get oranges. They had to send people to Guangzhou or Hong Kong to buy fruit for Mr. Zhang. Mrs. Zhang was not choosy about her fruit. My father ate oranges bought in Changsha.

The weather in Chengzhou was very depressing with its constant fog and humidity. Mr. Zhang refused to eat brown rice, only eating white rice, so he was vitamin B deficient. As a result, his legs became swollen. He was always in a very bad mood. During the few months in Chengzhou, he rarely went out and only occasionally went to the town.

Since the beginning of the war with the Japanese, and as time went by, Mr. Zhang got more and more depressed. He felt that his chances to participate directly in the war for his side were less and less. His power to influence political events diminished with every passing year.

Once, when Mr. Zhang walked down the street with my father and several plainclothes agents, an officer walked toward them. He suddenly stood in front of Mr. Zhang and saluted in attention and called out, "Deputy Commander!" Mr. Zhang looked at him and said nothing. My father saw that the officer was tall and big and wore the uniform of a Nationalist Lieutenant Colonel.

Immediately after returning, my father asked his agents to investigate the man and found out he was a deputy head of an artillery regiment stationed nearby. The regiment was the Northeast Army, whose men were still loyal to Zhang Xueliang. The entire regiment was ordered to be transferred to Hunan to fight the Japanese.

My father's orders were to not allow Zhang Xueliang to commit suicide, escape, or be rescued. Although Mr. Zhang was often in a bad mood, he was not the kind of person who would commit suicide. He would not escape, because the road was full of refugees and wounded soldiers, and he would not join the masses. Therefore, my father's main concern was that some people would attempt to rescue Zhang Xueliang. The manpower of the Northeastern artillery was five times that of ours, and it would be enough to rescue him.

However, my father could not permit Zhang Xueliang to be rescued. Even an attempt would force my father to take an action that he never wanted to take. His orders were that Zhang Xueliang could not be rescued alive.

To avoid that possibility, and because the regiment was still there, my father told Mr. Zhang in the evening that we would move out the next morning.

In the night, Suxianguan stepped up their alert. My father dispatched three special agents disguised as civilians to watch the front and around the camp of the artillery regiment. Their job was to observe any unusual movements of the soldiers.

The next morning, my father and his whole group "escaped" to Yongxing (永興), more than forty miles from Suxianling.

Yongxing was my father's hometown. Mr. Zhang, Mrs. Zhang, and a handful of agents stayed in the Ancestral Building, or "citan" (祠堂) run by the Liu family.

My father sent telegrams to ask for advice. A few days later Dai Li ordered them to move to Yuanling.

Chapter Four

YUANLING, HUNAN:
MARCH 1938 - LATE SEPTEMBER 1939

The first time I met Mr. Zhang, I was five years old, and my mother took myself and my two brothers to live with our father in Yuanling, Hunan (湖南沅陵).

In Yuanling, Mr. Zhang lived in the Fenghuang Temple of Fenghuang (Phoenix) Mountain. It was across the Yuan River diagonally opposite the city. At Mr. Zhang's request, the city government built a pagoda-like structure (a wangjiang tower, 望江樓), for him outside the temple. Mr. Zhang went there often with Mrs. Zhang to enjoy the river view.

My mother, myself, and my two brothers lived within walking distance to Fenghuang Mountain. We could see Yuanling City across the river, a pile of gray and black dwarf houses. Our rented houses were on the waterfront, in a rectangular row of three, facing the river with lawns reaching the beach. Fishing boats worked on the river, and ospreys stood in the water. From time to time, I watched the birds dive into the water and come up with big fish in their large beaks. The fishermen would take the big fish from the ospreys and exchange it for two small fish (the birds could only swallow small fish due to a small ring-like structure around their necks).

Cargo boats also sailed through the river. I still remember the wind blowing through the dark brown sails, wavy lines along the side of the boats, sailing fast and stable.

Men sold radishes on the beach, carrying a basket and calling "two pieces for one copper coin!" (一個銅版兩塊!) Whenever someone wanted to buy some, the men took out two radishes the size of a baby's palm and sprinkled them with hot red pepper.

My second eldest brother Philip, then seven years old, sometimes showed me how to fight the "Japanese devils" in our front beach. He used a pile of sand to make a tank and inserted a tree branch as a big gun pointed to the east where the Japanese Army was.

When an air raid alert sounded, people in the city crossed the river with a ferry boat to our side. A large group of people would stand on the beach and wait until the alarm was cleared before returning to the city. I once saw a man with a half-shaved head and the other half had hair pointed toward the sky, straight and black.

My big brother Bohan, then nine years old, and Philip were naughty. I just followed what they did. To punish us, my mother would make us kneel in a line in front of the bed. Only I was allowed to get up and call my father. He would ask our mother to let us up. Our father never raised his voice at us, but our mother occasionally made us "eat chestnut"—with her middle finger bent, she knuckled the top of our heads!

Zhang Yanfo (張嚴佛), the second in charge under Dai Li, was in Yuanling at that time. He often visited Mr. Zhang. His family and our family were close friends. His beautiful daughter Zhang Jingjing (張晶晶) and we three brothers often played together. My big brother was handsome, and Philip was smart, but Jingjing (who was about five years old) only took my little fat hand, ran around on the grass, and shouted that she would marry me. At least that's what my big brother told me. (Unfortunately, I can't remember it myself!).

Mr. Zhang always went out to the mountain and the river. He often sat on a large bamboo raft and directed somebody to pole it up and down the river using a long bamboo. He liked to hire a boat to fish on the river.

One day, my mother invited Mr. and Mrs. Zhang to our house for lunch. She set a round table outside the door facing the river because there was no room inside the house. My mother cooked many dishes that filled the whole table, and several people stood around it to eat.

After they left, my mother said to the empty table, "I did what I had to do. This should last for one year!" I always remembered this statement, but I didn't know what it meant. Now I know that my mother had to help Father entertain Mr. and Mrs. Zhang, and it was a big effort.

My brother Philip remembered more of that time than me. He wrote the following:

> That was in Phoenix Mountain in Yuanling, Hunan. The large dining room was brightly lit. Zhang Xueliang put his feet on the table and told jokes. One day, someone suddenly came in and said

Song Ziwen (宋子文) (Madame Chiang's brother) was here to see Mr. Zhang.

Everybody scattered. Mr. Zhang went outside to wait. Only I stood there like a fool (I was six or seven years old). Mr. Zhang waved me away. At this time, I saw one person coming, tall and dressed like a big shot. It must have been Song Ziwen. I did not hear what they said, but Mr. Zhang suddenly became very sad.

My brother and I never found out why he was sad or what they talked about.

Figure 6 l to r: Song Ziwen, Mrs. & Mr. Zhang

In Xiangxi (湘西), there were many bandits, and the garrison command headquarters in Yuanling was responsible for eliminating them. The commander-in-chief had been the head of a large bandit group before he changed sides. After he captured the bandits, an executioner would publicly behead them at a location on the beach near our house.

Once there was an execution, my big brother Bohan was very brave. He squeezed into a large circle of people in front to see the action. The executioner waved a long knife, chopped off the head of the bandit, and sent it several yards to the front. Immediately, several people rushed to the head and dipped steamed bread in the blood of the beheaded head and ate the bread. They believed that this would chase away evil and cure their diseases.

After Bohan came back, my mother beat him very hard. After that, we were not allowed to leave the house when there was an execution.

According to Deputy Xu Jianye (許建業), Xiangxi had a lot of bandits. When he went there to find a place for our group to live, it just happened that more than a thousand bandits attacked Yuanling city. They couldn't get into the city but disarmed the security patrols outside the city.

After Mr. Zhang had lived in Fenghuang Mountain for a year-and-a-half, the garrison commander of the city told Deputy Xu that he had information that the bandits were going to attack the city for a second time. But we also had to consider the possibility they might attack us, even though we lived on the other side of the river.

Fenghuang Mountain is located on the edge of the river, looking down the river. It was easy to defend but difficult to attack. My father and the military police commander planned to build a shelter, send people into it to defend the position, and close the road to the mountains.

When Mr. Zhang learned of this, he became excited and took over the command. His idea was to use rolling rocks and tree trunks for defense. The deputy commander-in-chief of the Chinese Air, Sea, and Air Forces, a three-star general, led a group of special agents and military police to place rocks and tree trunks at the critical high point that he pointed out.

Mr. Zhang used to love to play ghosts and tricks with those agents in their twenties. This time it was for real!

It was a pity that the bandits never showed up.

General Zhang Xueliang was disappointed he couldn't test his defensive strategy.

But we did encounter the bandits later.

When we moved from Yuanling to Guizhou, our fleet traveled through the mountains of Xiangxi. We were on the road through the valley in the evening, when, suddenly, many torches appeared on the mountain and surrounded us.

Normally, a commercial vehicle or military vehicle beset by bandits would stop and wait to be robbed, and the bandits would not kill anyone.

What did we do? We kept driving, with four dozen big guns (German-made Mausers) and several machine guns, all blasting toward the torches.

The torches on the mountain immediately and completely extinguished!

They had never faced such dense firepower before.

At the time, the bandits liked the big guns. The chiefs had to have one. If it was a large group, there might be more than one big gun for the small headman. The smaller groups only had single shot rifles, firearms, or long knives. When they heard the blasts of so many big guns, they knew they could not handle us! They didn't know that General Zhang Xueliang was sitting in a car and had closed his eyes to rest.

Chapter Five

XIUWEN, GUIZHOU:
OCTOBER 1939 TO MAY 1941

From October 1939 to May 1941, Zhang Xueliang lived in Yangming Cave (陽明洞) in Xiuwen, Guizhou (貴州修文), the place where an ancient scholar, Wang Yangming (王陽明), lived in exile during the Ming Dynasty. The compound included the Yangming Academy on the top of the cave and two wooden buildings in the courtyard. There was a gentleman's pavilion and other houses outside the Academy. The gentleman's pavilion contained many rooms where people could live.

Mr. Zhang, Mrs. Zhang, his bodyguard, Du Fa (杜發, who Mr. Zhang called "Old Du," and who we called Deputy Du) and her maid, Wang Ma (王媽)[5] lived in the upper floors of the wooden building in the courtyard. The first room downstairs was where Mr. Zhang bathed, and the second room was where everyone ate.

---

5. We referred to Mrs. Zhang's maid as "Wang Ma," which translates to "Mother Wang," or "Mom Wang." It was a common and familiar way to address adults in our household.

My father lived upstairs on the right side in the courtyard. The main hall in the courtyard was where people read newspapers and played chess. Deputy Xu Jianye and some agents also lived in the Academy. The other agents lived in the gentleman's pavilion, while the military police lived further out.

Figure 7 Mr. and Mrs. Zhang Yu Fengzhi

Mr. Zhang's bodyguard, Du Fa, was a big man from the Northeast. He had a bearish back, long arms extending over his knees, and oversized palms. I thought he walked like a gorilla. He was an expert in martial arts; a dozen people couldn't get near him.

But he couldn't shoot very well; his fingers were too thick!

He was always around Mr. Zhang, except when he ate or slept.

Du Fa was once the bodyguard of Mr. Zhang's father, Zhang Zuolin. The old man reluctantly gave his best bodyguard to protect his son.

Mr. Zhang had another bodyguard, Aide Li, who lived in a single room near the Pavilion. He kept all of Mr. Zhang's games, such as chess, a horse-racing board game, and the like. Mr. Zhang used to play a children's horse racing game with us. We threw dice and moved the horse according to the throw we got. I was the one who went to Aide Li to get the game and return it after we played.

Aide Li played tennis very well. He was my father's partner when they played doubles with Mr. Zhang. His partner was an agent who could hold a tennis racket.

Aide Li was a tall, slim, and cold man. He was a martial arts expert who never missed his target when he shot a revolver, a crack shot (百發百中).

Because Mr. Zhang already had a bodyguard, my father decided to keep only one. When we left Xiuwen in 1942, Aide Li was sent to the Military Control Bureau (軍統局) in Chongqing. The boss Dai Li said to "lock him up," so he was jailed at the Bureau.

He was imprisoned because he knew too much: Zhang Xueliang's daily routine, his activities, and the strength and arrangement of Father's group. These could not be known to outsiders.

In 1949, when the Military Control Bureau decided to withdraw from Chongqing to Taiwan, Aide Li was executed. What a high price he paid to be Mr. Zhang's bodyguard!

Master Chef Chen of Mr. Zhang's kitchen was Sichuanese, but he knew how to prepare a delicious pasta. Mr. Zhang's dinner table was rectangular. Usually, my father and Deputy Xu accompanied Mr. and Mrs. Zhang to eat. Our mother and the kids would eat at the same table if we were there. The waiter Ami served us. Du Fu, Mr. Zhang's bodyguard and personal servant, and Wang Ma, Mrs. Zhang's personal maid, ate in other rooms. The other agents ate at a mass kitchen.

Mr. Zhang's lunches and dinners were very rich. Besides the shared dishes, each person had a small dish of butter in front of them, which was used for steamed bread. For lunch, Mr. Zhang sat at the head of the table. After he ate his lunch, he went upstairs to take his nap.

At dinner, it was different. He always talked about various subjects or jokes. He talked loudly, and others listened and laughed. I remember once Deputy Xu laughed so hard that he fell backwards to the ground, because he had put his feet on the table. This was a big fall: my father transferred him back to the Bureau—putting his feet on the table was not respectful to Mr. Zhang. Also, he gave a gun to Mr. Zhang when they drove to Huangshan. In order to please Mr. Zhang, he had forgotten his responsibilities and duties.

They ate American canned fruit after dinner. Mr. Zhang asked me what I wanted. I replied that I wanted the ones with a hole in it. This was Hawaiian canned pineapple, where each slice had a hole in the center.

Mr. Zhang liked to go fishing. Xiuwen did not have a large river. He could only fish in streams or ponds near the mountain.

Sometimes he took a bamboo sedan chair and went fishing in the river far away. At noon, the bearers took rice porridge and steamed bread to them for a picnic.

After eating, Mr. Zhang would lay face up on a large rock and sunbathe his big belly.

The agents gave him a nickname: "big fat man," but they only dared to call him this behind his back.

Mr. Zhang called me "little fat boy" (小胖子). That became my nickname for years to come.

My mother took us boys to live in Xiuwen city.

I hadn't started school yet, so I often lived with my father at the compound. I played alone and sometimes wandered into Mrs. Zhang's room. She was very nice to me and talked to me kindly and gave me candy. Wang Ma was also very nice to me. She was short and crippled, with a lot of wrinkles on her face. Mrs. Zhang hired her not for her abilities as a maid, but to repay an old favor.

In the evening, the big bodyguard Du Fa and some of the young agents often chatted in the courtyard farthest away from Mr. Zhang's room. Once, Du Fa held a pack of popped rice candy out in his big hand for me to eat. He made me drink a glass of water before giving me a piece of candy. As a result, I drank four glasses of water and ate four pieces candy.

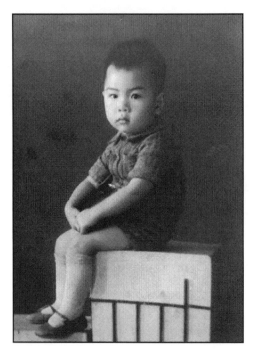

Figure 8 The author at age 3 or 4 in Nanjing

That night, I wet my father's bed. I remember he hung the bed sheet himself in the dark.

In February 1942, Mrs. Zhang got cancer and brought Wang Ma with her to the United States. Her personal aide Yu also left us. He didn't go with her to the United States; he was free to go and married later in mainland China. The two bodyguards, Du Fa and Aide Li of Zhang Xueliang were not so lucky; as noted above, Li was executed, and Du Fa later hanged himself.

Zhao Yidi (趙一荻), who we called Miss Four, came to Xiuwen to replace Mrs. Zhang in February 1942 and began her 72-year-long relationship with Mr. Zhang. She brought her personal maid, Wu Ma (吳媽), with her.

After Mrs. Zhang arrived in the United States, she sent me a wool suit with shorts.

I later ran into Mrs. Zhang again in Los Angeles in 1963. I had come to study in the United States and worked at the Peking Restaurant to earn my next semester's living expenses and tuition fees.

One day, the Northeastern Fellow Countrymen Association had a dinner party in the Peking Restaurant. They occupied about twenty tables, each seating eight or ten people. An elegant lady sat at the head of the head table. I immediately recognized her as Mrs. Zhang!

I was a waiter at that time, but that table was not assigned to me. Anyway, I rushed to her and served a cup of tea. I stepped back far away and took a deep bow toward her.

I silently said to myself, "Thank you!" I didn't know what I meant by it. It just came to my mind.

She did not look at me at all, not even a glance. She just sat there peacefully and enjoyed her own thoughts. She was as beautiful as a deity from the heavenly realm (仙女下凡). When she knew me, I was still a small child. Now that I was an adult, she certainly didn't recognize the "little fat boy" she once knew.

Chapter Six

GUIYANG, GUIZHOU:
MAY 1941 - FEBRUARY 1942

FIRST OPERATION

While in Xiuwen, on October 4, 1941, Zhang Xueliang suddenly suffered a severe stomach pain and thought that it was appendicitis. My father immediately accompanied him and Miss Four on the drive directly to Guiyang, the capital of Guizhou Province.

At the same time, he asked Deputy Xiong Zhongqing (熊仲青) to report the situation to "Boss" Dai Li, head of the Military Control Bureau.

Dai Li contacted the Governor of Guizhou, Wu Dingchang (吴鼎昌), to put his police chief Xia Song (夏松) in charge to help. Xia Song was a high-level agent of the Military Control Bureau, who was sent to take the position of Head of the Police Department of Guizhou.

Xia went to the Guiyang Central Hospital, the best in the capital and requested the hospital to prepare to receive an important patient.

The driver, Chen Asi (陳阿四), drove very well, able to change gears with his foot. The road was very bad, so he had to drive very slowly to make sure that Zhang Xueliang could endure the several hours riding in the car.

My father sent an advance team to the hospital. They set up traffic control, chased people from the hospital entrance, and got the operating room ready.

When Zhang Xueliang arrived, the dean and the chief surgeon's doctor were waiting at the door, and Zhang Xueliang was pushed directly to the operating room. After the operation, for security reasons, all the patients of the surgery department were moved out. No more operations would be performed for the several days Zhang Xueliang was there to recover.

My father did the right thing for Zhang Xueliang, but it was against the rules set up by his boss Dai Li. My father should have gotten permission from him before making any important decision. But my father couldn't stay at Xiuwen and wait for instructions when he had to call for emergency medical services for Zhang Xueliang.

My father knew this rule. Could he get away with it?

The "Boss" Dai Li was the Head of the Military Control Bureau, the spy service with more than 50,000 special agents under his control. They operated behind enemy lines and within the country, with many capable men and difficulties to handle. How did he do it?

He created a "family law." Every agent was a member of the family, and he was the father of this big family. He published the booklet "Family Rules" that was issued regularly. It talked about "leadership," "obedience," and "discipline." I read it once. But what really worked was his philosophy of three penalties:

1. Scold (骂),
2. Put in jail (關監牢), and
3. Execution (槍斃).

What he said counted. No trial was required. My father only had two penalties he could threaten:

1. Scold (骂), and
2. Put in jail (關監牢).

"I will put you in jail!" my father frequently said to some of his agents, but mostly it was just scolding. Of course, he did send a few to the Military Control Bureau's jail. The person would be told go to Chongqing (the headquarters) to turn himself in.

What my father said counted. No trial was required!

My father took Zhang Xueliang from the residence at Xiuwen without getting permission from Dai Li. That was against Dai Li's first rule.

After Zhang Xueliang went through the operation, Dai Li and my father sat in my father's office. The boss shouted at my father for a while and then told my father, "Take your gun out!"

My father took his revolver from his belt and put it on the table between them. "Take your gun out" usually meant he would be suspended! By putting his revolver on the table it meant he had to obey the order.

But that was not the time to suspend my father. He was told to stay. And Dai Li had to deal with Zhang Xueliang.

Dai Li came to the hospital to see Zhang Xueliang several times. Once, my father accompanied him to the ward to see him. Dai Li took out a Longines watch and gave it to Mr. Zhang as a gift. But Mr. Zhang took it and just gave it to my father. My father pretended he did not see the boss's embarrassed face; he put the watch in his pocket.

My father wore that watch for the rest of his life.

My brother Philip wrote the following about this event, which he remembers slightly differently:

"Mr. Zhang Xueliang had acute appendicitis. My father drove hundreds of miles to Guiyang for the operation and saved Mr. Zhang's life.

Dai Li once gave an expensive watch to Mr. Zhang (a Longines, a rarity during the war). Dai Li later went to see Zhang Xueliang and saw my father wear the Longines watch on his wrist. He asked my father, 'Where did you get this watch?'

Without changing expressions, he replied, 'Zhang Xueliang gave it to me.'

Zhang Xueliang gave that watch to my father. It was against the rules to accept it, but it was not proper to refuse it.

My father decided it would be better to wear it openly. Let the boss see it. This would avoid the agents making a 'small report' (every agent of the Bureau could report directly to the headquarters). Dai Li was very smart and alert. My father worked under him for twenty years because he did things correctly."

After the surgery, Zhang Xueliang was out of danger. The doctor said it was peritonitis. This operation was only an emergency one. After a recuperation period, he needed another surgery. After taking over the surgery ward of the Central Hospital for a few days, they didn't want to occupy the entire ward for too long. Since they couldn't immediately perform the operation, it was better to move out. They found a nearby nunnery that was suitable.

SECOND OPERATION

On the outskirts of Guiyang stands Qianling Mountain (黔靈山). The Kirin Cave (麒麟洞) was on the hill, a bodhisattva inside the cave, a nunnery outside the cave, and a lot of rooms. My father left Kirin Cave and a row of rooms near the end of the cave for the nuns to live in. He wrote a note, "Off limits to team members," and posted it to the entrance of the nuns' living quarters.

He rented all the other rooms for our group.

My father transferred some people from Xiuwen to Kirin cave. These included the Chief Chan, some members of the team including Jiang Youfang (a distant grandson of Chiang Kai-shek) and Zhong Ziwen (鍾子文, the accountant), and me. I accompanied my father because I hadn't started school yet. There, the accountant taught me to memorize the 9 x 9 multiplication table. I used it for many years when playing mahjong to compute my winnings.

In our living quarters, there was a row of four rooms on the right side of the entrance gate. Mr. Zhang and Miss Four lived in the farthest room, Wu Ma lived in the second room, the third room was the dining room, and the fourth room was for Du Fa.

My father and I lived in a single room on the left side of the entrance of the compound. The other people in the retinue lived behind the nuns' rooms.

During the New Year, the nuns gave us four dishes of snacks. Mr. Zhang gave them a lot of money in return. He said that the nuns "ate from four directions," meaning they got their meals from other people (吃四方的).

There were several fourteen-year-old nuns beside the middle-aged nuns. They were pale and expressionless. But during the Chinese New Year, they were permitted to gamble, and played games like "Pick the Lucky Number." I was the only "special agent" allowed to play with them, and I liked it. Those young nuns got excited; their pale faces filled with blood when they gambled. My "foreign capital" also was very welcomed.

Several decades later, one nun I gambled with wrote a memoir about Zhang Xueliang's stay in their place. She would be over ninety years old now. I wonder how she is.

After Zhang Xueliang recuperated, the chief surgeon Yang Jingbo (楊靜波) deemed Zhang Xueliang ready for the second operation. They decided to transfer the surgery facility to our place to operate there. He would take two very capable surgeons to assist as he operated.

My father asked for two doctors who were present the last time to assist this operation. Dr. Yang replied, "I've scheduled the best surgeons who work under them. The patients scheduled for operation by them were filled for weeks."

My father said, "In that case, we will take Zhang Xueliang to the hospital to operate, and we want the two original doctors."

Dr. Yang said quickly, "We will come there! We will come!" He was afraid we would take up the entire surgical department again.

My father's thinking was that in the first operation, Zhang Xueliang's life depended on the doctors' hands, and it turned out well. If they changed the doctors for the second operation, the unknown factor would increase.

Later, Zhang Xueliang himself said about his operation, that someone wanted to buy a doctor to kill him on the surgeon table.

So, our dining room was converted to a surgical room. All the doors and windows were covered with wet paper, and charcoal stoves were placed inside to turn the room into a steam room. The three surgeons operated on Zhang Xueliang. With sweat all over their faces, the operation was very successful and quick. If it took too long, they would have all cooked.

Zhang Xueliang had to remain in Guiyang for a few months, under the doctors' observation, to recover completely.

For the next four months, Zhang Xueliang quietly and peacefully recovered from the operation, not going out anywhere. The three doctors often came to check him. They all wore suits and ties. They played bridge with Zhang Xueliang. For a country boy like me, I thought they were good doctors.

At that time, Miss Four began to have a toothache. Agent Jiang Youfang always accompanied her to the dentist in Guiyang City. They always took me with them as a chaperone. The reward was a large piece of American candy given to me by Miss Four.

During this period, Mr. Zhang and my father got along the best. Mr. Zhang and Miss Four played Hunan "Run Hu" (湖南跑胡) with my father and me. Hunan "Run Hu" is a card game printed with simple numbers, one, two . .

. nine (一, 二 . . . 九) and another group printed in "big writing" (大写), one, two . . . nine （壹, 貳 . . . 玖). The same word had four cards each.

The method of play is like mahjong, where each player gets thirteen cards, and the dealer gets fourteen cards. To win, you try to make four sets of three, either of the same card, or in sequence, and another pair of the same. Because the number of cards is small (72 compared to the 136 tiles in mahjong), it was easy to know who needed which card. Miss Four played according to the best way. My father wouldn't try to help me. Only Mr. Zhang liked me, "the little fat boy," so he always fed me the card I needed to let me win some money.

I really didn't know who was trying to please who.

I was a country boy come to the city. For the first time in my life, I ate bananas and watched movies. Jiang Youfang took me to see the movie, "Mulan Joins the Army." (木蘭從軍). I still remember that the heroine sang, "Where is the moon? Which village has the moon?" (月亮在哪裡? 月亮在哪鄉?).

The second time, he took me to see the martial arts movie "Huang Tianba" (黃天霸). After I came back, Mr. Zhang stopped me in the hallway and asked me what movie I watched. I said, "Big Huang Tianba." Mr. Zhang threw me a funny look and said, "Huang Tianba is Huang Tianba! How did you come out with the Big Huang Tianba?"

When we were in Guiyang, my mother's younger brother, Uncle Mao, would visit us. He was the child of my grandfather and our maid. My mom liked Uncle Mao very well. He treated us well. He worked with my father in Guiyang and always invited us to eat "hot pot," (a meal where we jointly cooked items in boiling soup), the only thing he could afford. We always put heavy wheat dough into the boiling water.

Later, Zhang Xueliang recovered completely. Guiyang was bombed intensely by the Japanese, and Zhang Xueliang's residence was no longer a secret. Dai Li decided to move them to Liuyu Village in Kaiyang County (開陽縣 劉育鄉).

Chapter 7

LIUYU VILLAGE, KAIYANG COUNTY, GUIZHOU:
FEBRUARY 1942 – WINTER 1944

Liuyu Village? I hadn't heard of it. We lived there for three years. We only heard that it was called "Liuya." Only Dai Li could find this remote and backward countryside for Zhang Xueliang to live.

Here is what my brother Philip wrote:

> Watch Zhang Xueliang, be kind, be suicide prevention, and prevent him from being hijacked. The latter may be the reason why Zhang Xueliang was trapped in Guizhou for a long time. At that time, Guizhou was the only province in the rear that was not controlled by local forces. Even so, my father's team still needed to make a lot of arrangements to prepare for Zhang Xueliang.
>
> The retinue consisted of a spy team of more than thirty people, a gendarme (100+ people), and a nearby guard group of over three hundred

people. They also arranged the officers of the Military Control Bureau to serve as the mayor of the counties we stayed in [Wang Chongwu (王崇武)for Xiuwen, Li Yuzhen(李毓楨) for Kaiyang County].

Deputy Xiong (Xiong Zhongqing) was the captain of the Kaiyang County city security police. He sent some agents to open a grocery store at the gate of the city. He arranged it carefully, solemnly.

I remember that it seemed to be in Liuyu Village, Kaiyang County. My father took two of our brothers—two primary school students—each carrying a box of guns (a barge gun). It was the three of them who went to the county office to visit the headman.

He took his children as guards, came to the door of the local government, as a way to threaten with no threats. He had to try very hard.

My father was really a spy captain, and he was full of tricks! My two brothers were only eleven and nine years old. I can just imagine the proud look on big brother Bohan's face at that time.

Liuya was a rice-based rural area with inconvenient transportation. The road ended and cars could not go there.

Most of the village residents had the last name Liu. The Liu's Ancestral Hall was there.[6] Dai Li had arranged to build the houses near there for us to live. They were several rectangular wooden structures. We also rented the Ancestral Hall for agents to live in.

What I remember clearly is the restroom, in the back of the house. The restroom had bamboo walls, a straw roof,

---

6. Liu is the family name of the Han Dynasty (30 emperors of the Han Dynasty had the last name Liu).

and a pit in the ground with two boards to squat on. The flies flew all over my head. The pit was full of fat white maggots, piled up and moving.

Guizhou people were really smart. In order to collect human waste for fertilizer, they put a "free" public toilet in the paddy field. It certainly was a large toilet, about 2.5 cubic meters (2.5 meters on each side and high, set over a 2.5 meter diameter round hole in the ground).

They built two long wooden bars about two meters above the ground, one larger and one smaller; both were very smooth. It was installed in such a way that you could sit on one bar with your bare butt and the smaller one served as a handrail. To get to your position, you sat on one bar and used the handrail to pull yourself over.

Once, Father and our three brothers sat in a row. My father pulled himself to the furthest end, my two big brothers followed, and I sat near the entrance. We all sat and held the handrail in front of us, and I hugged the handrail with my short arms.

The breeze came through the bamboo wall. There was no stinging smell, no flies, and no maggots. We sat on the bar in the middle of the air, enjoying ourselves.

Then a teenage servant came through a hole in front of us on the ground level, digging up manure. He didn't look up.

We didn't say hello either.

In Liuya, we used a vegetable oil lamp, where we put the oil in a small dish, with three or five lamp wicks. The brightness was about three or five watts, or candle lights. Mr. Zhang used kerosene lamps. Its brightness was about ten watts.

Mr. Zhang told us a joke:

"There is a miser, and when he dies, he refuses to close his eyes. He lies in his coffin with one finger pointing upward. What was wrong? His youngest son knew his father, who was miserly even in death. It was because there were three wicks in the lamp placed in front of the coffin. The son takes out two of the wicks out from the lamp, leaving only one. Their father lowers his finger and closes his eyes!

Then, before they close the coffin, the eldest son puts five yuan in the coffin to show his final respects. The second son, who is both filial and clever, writes a ten yuan 'I owe you' note, places it in the coffin, and takes out the five yuan in cash. The youngest son writes a fifteen-yuan IOU note, places it in the coffin, and takes out the ten-yuan IOU."

The water pulled from the well was not clean. Drinking water was filtered with sand: a wooden barrel with coarse sand, fine sand, and charcoal and palm leaves were layered from top to bottom. The water was poured on it, and the water that flowed out to the bamboo faucet below was filtered.

It could be drunk as it was, but waiter Ami boiled the water and placed it in a thermos to serve to Mr. Zhang.

My mother took us to live in a large courtyard owned by a landlord, Liu Huaqing (劉華清). The courtyard had three sides with rooms. The last side had a wall separating the living quarters from the garden. The center of the court was covered with sandstone slabs.

The entrance was a large hallway; there was a swallow nest on the door. In the spring, the mother flew in with worms in her beak. Three baby swallows stuck their heads out and opened their little beaks, making a sound like *ge ge ge*.

We rented the rooms on both sides. The main house in the center was occupied by the landlord Liu Huaqing. He was in his sixties and was very smart and fit. He was a widower, and he kept a beautiful young maid Ciulan (翠蘭) to serve him. His two sons our age studied in Kaiyang. When they came back on vacation, they played with us in the courtyard. We played "Hold Your Goose Egg" under the moonlight.

During the Lunar New Year, Liu Huaqing slaughtered a pig in the courtyard. He distributed the meat to his peasant tenants. The tenants only ate meat three times a year, during the New Year, planting, and harvesting.

They killed the pig by placing a low table in the middle of the courtyard, put on a large pot of boiling water, and four people pressed the pig on the table. One person with a long knife pierced it from the neck to the heart, and the blood flowed out into a tub, the pig screaming loudly, as its blood ran out. Then a person cut a hole in the leg and inserted a hollow bamboo tube through to the ear. The person blew air through the bamboo tube until the pig skin expanded to form a balloon, and then they lifted the pig to the boiling water pot. Two individuals shaved the bristles on the back, to save to make toothbrushes.

The cleaned and shaven pig would be cut open and cut into pieces and distributed to the waiting tenant peasants. The liver and blood were kept by the landlord.

Li Feizhang (李斐章) told me that some twenty years after the Communists took over, Liu Huaqing was publicly judged by his tenant peasants, pronounced guilty, and executed for being a landlord.

Not far from where we lived, there was a permanent place for a farmers market every Sunday. It was a long grass shed

51

with no walls and empty booths on both sides. The first one on the left held an urn, usually empty. I sometimes went there to find sparrow eggs on the roof.

Everyone came to the market: the farmers with vegetables, the blacksmith, and the sellers for cloth and daily necessities. The people from several nearby villages came to buy things. It was very crowded.

At the end of the booth, my father added a parking garage with a door. Mr. Zhang's black sedan parked there. The biggest attraction for visitors was to "see the car." They went to the door to look at the car parked inside. That was the first time in their lives they saw a car.

The team did not buy food here. Every day, they sent someone to Kaiyang to buy food.

Mr. Zhang had a rectangular table in the dining room. Lunch and dinner were served there by waiter Ami. If I had breakfast there, Ami served me two fried eggs. He always put some soy sauce on it. Mr. Zhang and Miss Four ate their breakfast in their room. Ami served them western style breakfasts.

The kitchen for Mr. Zhang was on a separate mud platform. Master Chef Chan was always there. When I was there, I often went to the kitchen. When the master chef made bread, I used his dough to make a rabbit.

Once, I looked at the Jinhua ham on the wall and I said, "Master Chef, the ham is for eating, not for hanging on the wall."

The master chef played a special agent for a change. He reported me to Zhang Xueliang, who laughed until he was out of breath.

People never seemed to get sick. There was no doctor in the countryside anyway.

I remember when some of our fellow Hunan chair bearers got "fire eyes" (deep red eyes), they came to my mother. She gave them her secret formula, "Huanglian Bingpian" (黃蓮冰片), to wash their eyes.

And it worked!

I started elementary school at that time. At the end of the year, I got a C. According to the school rules, I could move up to second grade, but mother told me to remain in first grade.

Our school was an old temple. In the woods on a hill, every morning I saw a few towering trees behind the flagpole. Several big birds proudly stood on the top of the trees.

We all walked to school. It didn't snow in winter, but it was very cold. The students wore straw shoes. Only my brother Philip and I wore cloth shoes. The students each carried a piece of charcoal, six inches long. I carried a longer one. After arriving in the classroom, we started a fire under our table on the dirt floor to keep ourselves warm. After class, everyone squatted under the table and made popcorn.

At noon in the summer, we snuck into a small river to swim, everyone naked, doing the dog paddle.

Between classes, we played ball in the classroom. The ball was made with string rolled into a ball. It could only be bounced once. The person who got the ball hit it against the wall above the blackboard.

Only I had a rubber ball that could bounce more than once; it was a Yong brand ball (永字牌). One day when I played alone, the ball rolled to the pond in the field. I walked over and picked up the ball, saw a few small waves on the surface of the water. Some insects stood on the surface, with long legs and long wings, one skating over the surface, leaving a fan-shape wave behind.

I asked myself: Where did they come from? Where did they go after the pond dried up?

Chapter Eight

LIUYU VILLAGE:
February 1942 - Winter 1944

When the students came home from school, they some-times went into the woods to pick dead branches for their stoves. I once went with them, picked up a small dead tree, carried it on my shoulder and went home. After seeing it, my mother smiled sadly and told me, "Don't do that again."

We used a stove made from mud, with two large openings, one on the top, another in front. We placed a big iron pot on the hole on top. We cooked everything in that pot; it just stayed there, because it was too heavy to lift.

In the big hole in front, we put in large pieces of cut up wood and some grasses, squatted down, and blew with a bamboo tube until the smoke and fire came up and our tears came down.

The crispy-cooked rice cake at the bottom of the iron pot was delicious. I often put some in my pocket, walking and eating; that was the only snack I could have.

In Liuyu Village, we picked our own fruit from the trees.

I developed the ability to climb trees, which benefitted my teenage years.

Liuyu Village's soil was very poor. Apples grew to the size of cherries, mangos the size of my big toe, and wild grapes the size of soybeans. There was a kind of thorn pear on the roadside, like a cockroach with white thorns. Small animals couldn't bite it because there was no place to put their mouth, so it was left to us. Only we could pick it and eat them. We had fingers, you know!

Mr. Zhang also went to pick wild grapes to make wine. He put a layer of sugar on a layer of grapes and let it ferment.

We also went to a forest full of red bayberry trees on the roadside. I tasted it and spit it out. It was too sour.

Mr. Zhang was very intelligent. He must have known that if there was a tree full of plums on the roadside, then the plums must have been sour.

So why then would Zhang Xueliang still return many times? Because there was no place else to go!

NEW YEAR'S GAMBLING

The Lunar New Year were happy days for everyone. My father let everyone gamble.

Mr. Zhang gave us children each a red envelope on New Year's Eve to gamble.

Figure 9 l to r: Zhang Xueliang, Deputy Xiong
Zhongqing, Platoon Leader Zhang

Mr. Zhang, Miss Four, and my entire family were the
core players, and Deputy Xiong also participated. We
played five-card stud poker. We played at the dining table,
so for five or ten minutes, we would leave the table to wait
for it to be set up. Miss Four would throw the dice with us
kids. This would last for fifteen days until the Festival of
the Lanterns.

My father gave agents five days to gamble. He played
a few hands of the simplest game with them. The agents
could hardly wait for my father to leave. Then they played
for real.

Once they passed the fifth day, they still sneaked some
play in.

My father took a stout stick, waving it kung fu style at
the door, pretending to rush in. The Special Agents jumped
out the window. My big brother Bohan crawled under the
bed.

Don't worry! My father's stick had eyes and it wouldn't hit people!

My father got a nickname from the agents as "the German" or "Hitler," though of course, not just for this event.

PAI GOW

Pai gow is a game with thirty-two tiles. The dealer sits on one side of a table. Players sit or stand on the right, left or opposite side of the dealer. Players place bets. The dealer deals two tiles to each player. The players turn their tiles, the points are shown, and then the dealer turns up his tiles.

The dealer and the player compare points. Points are added from the two tiles. If they add up to ten or more, ten points are subtracted. Therefore, ten is zero.

Or, based on the pair's rank, any pair is higher than the combination of numbers.

Wins or losses are paid, and the bets taken away. It is that simple.

WE BET ON "LONG DRAGON"

When a player puts two coins, one overlaid on the other (one cent or one yuan or any value the dealer allowed), he or she makes a "long dragon" bet.

It means you bet on all seventeen ranks of the two tiles. It will be paid according to the points you get: 1-to-1 for four- and five-point hands, 2-to-1 for eight-point hands,

3-to-1 for nine-point hands, and up to 17-to-1 for the highest pair. But if the dealer gets the winning hand, the players have to come up with the money according to the same odds.

Once Zhang Xueliang played with the agents, he asked me to sit next to him. We were on the left side of the dealer. Mr. Zhang always placed a "long dragon" bet with a 1-cent copper coin.

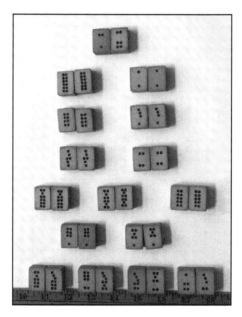

Figure 10 Pai gow tiles, pairs in rank order

The dealer was a high-ranking agent, Li Hongtu (李鴻圖). He was playing well and got very lucky. He won a lot of money (which was okay), but he got very arrogant (which was not okay).

Mr. Zhang told me, "I am going to wipe him out." He told me to bet all my money when he pulled one coin from his "long dragon" and left one coin on the table.

Then we played as usual. The big fat man got two tiles.

He handed one to me, the little fat boy. If he got tiles worth three to five points, he would have called out "細小歪斜斷" which meant Small Skew, or a four- or three-point tile. If I got one of those, I would shout "coming" and hit the table with my tiles face up.

If he got an eight, he would call "虎頭" (Tiger Head, or eleven points) or "金瓶" (Golden Bottle, or ten points). If he got a nine, he would call "金瓶大五" (Golden Bottle Big Five, or all ten points). If I got the right tiles, I would shout and hit the table with my card face up.

We played like this for a while. Then Mr. Zhang took one coin down from his "long dragon," and I bet all my money, and I won!

Then we waited for another right moment only Mr. Zhang could figure out. After I doubled and redoubled several times (still very little money), the other players got the idea. Some smart ones came to place bets on our side, following my lead.

Not long later, the dealer was wiped out.

Later, Mr. Zhang told us, he spent 400,000 silver yuan to learn the secret to playing pai gow! He explained that he played pai gow with a veteran. He kept losing and kept playing, and he was convinced that he would not always lose. For a long period, his loss accumulated to 400,000 silver yuan to the guru. This smart man finally taught Zhang Xueliang the secret of playing pai gow—how to figure out which hands were live and which were dead.

How much was 400,000 silver yuan?

Zhang Xueliang told a story. When the warlords fought each other, his father Marshal Zhang Zuolin sent some talented lobbyists to Shanghai to establish connections. He gave an envoy 400,000 silver yuan and sent him to Shanghai in the south to do the job. His only instructions were to give out favors with no strings attached.

Later, the special envoy came back, reporting to Marshal Zhang Zuolin that he had made very good connections. The deputies of warlord So-and-So had accepted his money, the concubines of warlord So-and-So had received his gifts, and so on. At the end he said, "Marshal, I have good news: I saved 40,000 silver yuan for you!"

The Marshal glanced at him and said, "You can't even spend 400,000 silver yuan? You are good for nothing!"

He waved him out and never used him again.

Young Marshal learned how to spend money from his father Zhang Zuolin, using and spending money throughout his life.

Chapter Nine

My mother often played mahjong with Zhang Xueliang and Miss Four. They played the simplest form, with thirteen tiles and few points, five points maximum. I remember that Mr. Zhang often said that "the tiles will flatter me."

My mother always said, "If you don't have enough suits, do not take a tile from others, it is better to get a tile from the deck." I follow this rule when playing mahjong. Every time my mother played mahjong, she asked me to put her pillow up on her bed. She thought this would help her win! Sometimes Kaiyang County Mayor Li Yuzhen (李毓楨, the mayor sent by Dai Li—wherever we lived, the mayor was replaced by a man loyal to Dai Li) played mahjong with Zhang Xueliang and deliberately made fun of my mother. For example, he'd tell Zhang Xueliang not to give her a tile or to intercept her tile, and Zhang Xueliang would laugh. And my mother would get angry and lose money. And I set up the pillow for nothing!

Zhang Xueliang enjoyed fishing in the pool or small river in the field. Once, when he was fishing, I was playing at a nearby rice field, and when I bent over to pick up something, I fell into the rice field headfirst. Mr. Zhang heard the splash and only saw my two chubby feet kicking in the air. He shouted and a nearby agent ran over and pulled me out of the mud.

At that time, Miss Four and Wu Ma were resting in a small pine forest nearby. The agent took me there. Wu Ma took off my clothes to dry under the sun. I sat on a pile of pine needles naked and waiting.

Zhang Xueliang saved my little life! It was fate!

DRY THE RIVER

Liuyu Village only had small creeks or ponds that were not easy for fishing.

Zhang Xueling said, "Dry the river!"

My father's men complied. They selected a section of the creek about three to four meters wide, built two dikes, twenty to thirty meters apart, and pumped out the water in between to dry the river. They first built a dike across the creek downstream, placed rocks to twenty centimeters below the water surface, and then placed gravel on its upstream face. That would let the water flow through but not the fish. Then they built a dike of rock and gravel upstream, thirty centimeters higher than the water surface. They placed some palm leaves on the gravel face, and then a layer of soil on the upstream face. This stopped the water flow.

Then, on the side of the river, two farmers' pumping trucks were used. Two Hunan bearers stepped on the pump to dry the river between the two dikes.

When the water got down to the level where we could see the backs of the fish, it was time to catch the fish.

The agents jumped in first, trying to use their martial arts skills to squeeze their hands around the fish, but the fish always slipped away.

The Hunan bearer, meanwhile, just gently put one hand under the fish belly, raised his hand under the fish, lifted his hand slowly, and threw the fish in the bucket he carried.

Once they found a lot of trout under the rocks; they got two buckets full. Now we know Americans like trout. We only liked carp, because the carp had no fish smell; only when they got to the United States did they smell bad.

Chapter Ten

MY MOTHER THE ENTREPENUER

During our twenty-five years of living and visiting with Zhang Xueliang during his house arrest, our family shared many meals with him. Throughout these meals, he liked to talk and talk loudly, so we heard many, many stories. When we all ate together, there would be seven or eight good dishes, mostly containing meat, which was expensive. He would finish eating quickly and would talk while the rest of us finished eating and listened.

Miss Four and our parents would eat slowly and listen to him. My brothers and sister would eat quickly and listen to him. It was a rare chance to eat meat, so I took advantage of this opportunity to eat quickly.

It was another matter for us when we ate at home alone without Mr. Zhang. Meat was very scarce and was never on the menu. In the ten years in the mainland, we children had to eat four or five bowls of rice along with a bowl of vegetables for our meals. We often ate boiled pumpkin (I won't eat pumpkins now). In Taiwan, the food improved. For the fifteen years in Taiwan, we ate four bowls of rice with a fish dish and a bowl of vegetables.

My Mother's Projects

My mother needed to make some extra money to put better food on the table. She was quite the entrepreneur. All my brothers looked like my father; I'm the only one who looked like my mother. My mother was very smart; she did a lot of business. She was "yitiaolong," or "one whole dragon"—she'd stretch all our resources to have more than one dish. These were some of her projects during the years in China:

Project 1: Raise Ducks

Around 1943 to 1944, when we were in Quezhou, my mother bought 200 baby ducks, and asked a ten-year old boy, Wang Shizhong (王世忠), the son of the Hunan sedan chair bearer (who we called Old Wang) to manage the ducks. During the day, Little Wang would chase the ducks into the rice paddy fields to find food. He used a long bamboo stick to direct the ducks. It had a bamboo spoon attached to the end, to scoop mud from the rice fields to throw in front of the ducks, to make them turn. Little Wang would sleep in the same hut with his duck troops at night. The Young Marshal Zhang give Little Wang the title of "Duck Captain." My mother's plan was to sell the eggs to make some money to support her family. Just as the ducks started laying eggs, we had to move to the city of Kaiyang so the kids could go to school, so she had to sell the eggs very cheaply and did not make the money she had hoped for.

PROJECT 2: MAKE POTATO NOODLES

When we moved to Kaiyang in 1944, my mother decided to buy a lot of potatoes to make potato noodles. The raw potatoes had to be blended into a semi-liquid pulp with a stone blender powered by a horse. So, my mother borrowed the only military horse from the captain of the company commanded by the military police under my father's control. Her recipe to make the noodles was: boil water in a large iron pot, pour the semi-liquid pulp into a sieve, and punch the pulp through the sieve into the pot to form the noodles. After cooking, the noodles would be hung up on a bamboo rod to dry. Unfortunately, before she could sell her noodles, we had to pack up and move to Guiyang.

PROJECT 3A: MAKE LIQUOR

We moved to the city of Tongzi (桐梓) so my two elder brothers could go to junior high school. We rented a courtyard with rooms on three sides, and a wall on the other side. My mother had to come up with another money-making plan. This time, she decided to make liquor from corn. Her plan was to:

> (1) Steam the corn grains with a big steamer; (2) add yeast in the cooked corn to ferment; (3) make a liquor steamer by stacking two large iron pots on top of each other in wooden circular barrels

one meter high; (4) put the fermented corn in the liquor steamer and boil the water in the lower pot; the steam would rise through the wooden barrel to reach the bottom of the iron pot at the top which was filled with cool water; (5) the liquor steam touching the cool bottom of the top pot would turn into liquor, flow along the bottom to the center into a bowl, which was connected to a tube that carried the liquor to a barrel on the ground.

The liquor was shipped to Guiyang in barrels, sold to alcohol factories to make pure alcohol to be used as fuel for trucks.

She sold the alcohol but didn't make money.

PROJECT 3B. RAISE PIGS

Evaporated distilled corn (a side product of the liquor-making process) was the best feed for pigs. So, my mother brought twenty baby pigs and fed them the distilled corn left over from making liquor. The distilled corn could be distilled once more to make liquor with less alcohol content that was enjoyed by many. But my mother, with her big heart, gave the second distillate to her baby pigs instead of making another liquor that she could have sold. The pigs grew quickly, but the anti-Japanese war was getting closer, and Zhang Xueliang had to move again.

My mother asked Deputy Xiong to chase the twenty pigs one hundred kilometers to Guiyang to sell them. The fat pigs walked very slowly, they had no food, and many just disappeared looking for food or died on the roadside. The pigs ran away to nearby farms, so the farmers were very happy to get new pigs! Within three or four days, no pigs were left. Deputy Xiong happily came back with no money for my mother's efforts.

In the end, none of her entrepreneurial ideas worked out, but she never stopped trying. My mother was very smart and always had ideas to try to make money.

She took care of the house based on the money my father gave us. Once, she asked my father to borrow more money. My mother said she couldn't handle the house anymore. I was about thirteen and cried, "Please continue to manage the house." My father said, "Okay, I will borrow more."

Chapter Eleven

TRAVELLING BY SEDAN CHAIRS AND CARAVAN

In the winter of 1944, the Japanese occupied Dushan, Guizhou (貴州獨山), so Dai Li ordered us to move from Kaiyang (we lived in Liuyu Village) to Tongzi, Guizhou (貴州桐梓).

At that time, only small cars like sedans or quarter-ton Jeeps could reach Liuyu, so he instructed us to go to Xifeng (息峰) to wait for the bus to pick us up. From Liuyu to Xifeng, there were more than a hundred miles of mountain road, and the only way to get there was to walk. My father followed his agents and service people walking. Mr. Zhang and Miss Four rode on sedan chairs (a chair borne by two bamboo poles carried by two people on their shoulders). The bearers were the four Hunan bearers who were with us, Long Fellow (長子), Big Wang (大老王), Little Wang (小老王), and Tan Jiayi (譚家易).

My mother held our little brother and rode in a sedan chair carried by two other Hunan bearers. My sister, one brother (my two elder brothers didn't come with us), Wu Ma, and I also took sedan chairs, but we were carried by hired local bearers.

I sat on the sedan chair, listening to the bearers echoing back and forth, I don't remember everything they sang. But I remember the front and rear bearers conveyed the road conditions to each other, and their music broke the loneliness of the silent empty mountains.

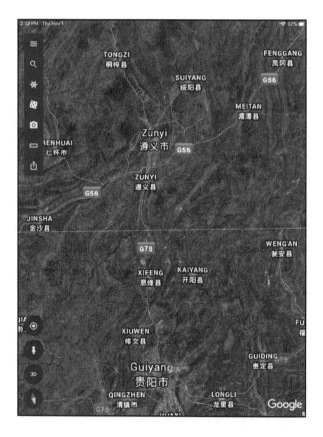

Figure 11 Map of area we lived in (Kaiyang, Tongzi)

The songs were poetic and practical. For example, the front one sang, "路邊兩朵花" or "there are two flowers on the roadside," meaning there were two women walking. The rear one would sing back, "千萬莫採他" or "No matter what, don't pick it," a warning to not touch them. The front ones would sing, "路邊一泡屎," or "there is a dump on the road," and the rear one would sing, "留給狗仔吃" or "leave it for the dog to eat." They meant they would not step on dog feces and to leave it for the dogs to eat (if everyone could think of taking care of wild dogs, the world would be in peace).

But Zhang Xueliang had more than seventy pieces of luggage that had to go with us, so we also used the caravan of Sichuan horses (川馬). One caravan consisted of thirty to forty horses. Two horses took the lead. The first one had five bells hung under his neck, and the second one had three. All the other horses walked in a single file following the lead horses. Each horse could carry two large pieces of rock salt (from the well mines of Sichuan, about fifty kilograms per piece) or other goods. The horses were thin and small, looked like donkeys, but had high endurance, most suitable for walking the mountain.

On the day of our departure, it was dawn and drizzling. We were all eating breakfast. I remember it was dry steamed bread. There were a group of Sichuan horses out in the open space. Many of them carried luggage. The ground was covered with luggage tied down with linoleum and hemp rope. There were more than one hundred pieces of luggage, mostly Mr. Zhang's. Zhang Xueliang did not need to bring furniture, pots, plates, or bowls, so what were those things?

Later, I learned that most of the items were calligraphy and paintings, as well as antiques from the Qing dynasty. When Zhang Zuolin and Zhang Xueliang were in power, they lived in Beijing. The palace eunuchs, or "taijian" (太監), who worked in the Emperor's palace had stolen treasures from the Qing Court. The taijian would first go to the big house (順承,Shuncheng Palace), where Zhang Xueliang and his father lived and worked, to sell them the wares because they had the money. The Zhangs would pay big money for the best ones. The ones they didn't want were later sold to the National Palace Museum. This resulted in the Zhangs having the best treasures. Eventually, when he was freed, Zhang Xueliang auctioned off the treasures internationally and made millions from them.

Concentration Camp

At the end of 1944, after arriving at Xifeng, the house being built for us in Tongzi was not yet finished. We had to temporarily stay in the concentration camp of the Military Control Bureau. Shortly before the New Year, Dai Li sent a medium-sized bus from Chongqing (重慶, the capital of China during the Sino-Japanese war, where the headquarters of the military was) to Xifeng for us.

The bus could fit about ten people. Zhang Xueliang was very satisfied after seeing it, but the truck hadn't arrived yet. The whole group couldn't go. It was a day's drive from Xifeng to Tongzi. My father decided to send my family first and have the bus come back for Mr. Zhang. He asked Jiang Youfang (蔣友芳), a relative of Chiang Kai-shek who eventually became Zhang Xueliang's manager after he was freed, to go with us, and we also took the Hunan bearer

Big Wang (大老王). It was a smart decision, because at the end of the trip, he had to carry my sister on his shoulder to walk several miles. We arrived at Tongzi and lived in the first two suites of the staff quarters of the concentration camp.

Jiang Youfang sent the bus back to Xifeng, but the bus went back to Chongqing, by order of Dai Li. He decided to move the group after the New Year.

I didn't know how Zhang Xueliang spent his New Year in the concentration camp.

But we had good time, Jiang Youfang changed a deck of new red cards, and we all played poker on New Year's Eve.

At the end of 1944, the Japanese had already reached the vicinity of Guiyang. The Sino-Japanese War was at the worst point for China. After the new year, Dai Li couldn't send the bus to Xifeng to pick up Zhang Xueliang. Instead, he sent some trucks for all of us.

Miss Four had to sit between the driver and Mr. Zhang. It was probably the only time in her life Miss Four rode a truck! After they arrived at Tongzi, Zhang Xueliang and my father had a big fight over this truck ride. My father told us that this was the second time they fought.

When my father took Zhang Xueliang from Liuyu to Tongzi, he didn't tell my brother Philip we were moving. He planned to tell him after we arrived. My father never left a forwarding address to anyone when we traveled due to safety concerns.

Philip was attending his first year of junior high school in Guiyang. When the Japanese hit the vicinity of Guiyang, the school closed and told each student to leave the dormitory. Philip went to Liuyu, the last place he knew our family stayed. But he didn't know we weren't there anymore.

Here are his recollections:

> Guizhou is part of the Yunnan-Guizhou Plateau. Everyone said of it that 'there is no three miles of flat land' and 'no one has three ounces of silver.' Sisters would share one pair of pants.
>
> Zhou Yichun (周詒春), the director of the Guizhou Education Department, was the head of Qinghua University. He gathered more than twenty graduates of Qinghua University in Huaxi, Guizhou, and opened a middle school, of course, called Qinghua Middle School (清華中學). Huaxi is more than fifty miles away from Guiyang, flowers and trees lined the creek, a wonderland's paradise. Six classes, more than two hundred students, with equal reputations to the Nankai Middle School (南開中學)and National Fourteen Middle School (for exiled students) (國立十四中).[7]
>
> I remember that year (1943), my father took my eldest brother and me to Guiyang to apply for Qinghua Middle School. However, we didn't get up in the morning and missed the first exam. Fortunately, a Qinghua teacher asked us to take the test during the second class. If our score was good, we could make up the exam. Later, I made up the exam and finally I could enter Qinghua Middle School in Guiyang. Big brother Bohan did not pass the exam, and he got a big spanking from my father. This was the big disadvantage of being the big brother in the family; he had to bear all the mistakes. (Note: After returning to Kaiyang, my

7 . In China, middle school included high school.

mother sent my big brother to Xiangyin, Hunan (湖南湘陰)for our grandfather to educate and discipline).

In the summer of the first year, I returned to Kaiyang's home and brought back a transcript with a comment from the first-grade tutor, 'Bad habits, deep rooted, and hopeless!' This stern commentary frightened my parents. In fact, I did have deeply rooted bad habits, because it was the first time I left home. I was homesick, and I'd lie on the grass reading. School was unbearable. The tutor was a man, and I was a pet of a female teacher.

There is a lot of talk, but I haven't said how I bumped into my father's Deputy Gong's team. Good things didn't last. I was less than a year in Huaxi Qinghua Middle School. One day, the teacher called everyone to the classroom and announced that the Japanese army had arrived at Sandouping, fifty kilometers from there. Everybody had to go home. (This reminds me of the story 'The Last Lesson' I read in elementary school. It was the second day of the war, when Poland was occupied by Germany, and the elementary school teacher finished the class. After that, he said to the students, "This is our last lesson!)

I carried a quilt on my back. I don't remember whether I walked or rode in a carriage. I went fifty miles outside of Guiyang to find my Uncle Mao (my mother's younger brother). He was a member of the Guiyang Guards Department and had just sent a truck to evacuate documents to send to Chongqing. He arranged for me to ride in the truck to go to Xifeng. At Xifeng, I went to the hotel where I used to live during summer vacation. The hotel was full of people who had fled the Japanese. The boss lady asked me if I had a quilt. I said yes, and she said, 'Sleep with me, your quilt is good for one more guest.

It really was not difficult to live, carrying a quilt on my back. I could go around the world!

The next day, I went to the hotel restaurant to eat. Deputy Gong's team was in the hall. He pointed to me and said, 'Do you know? Your father is with a large group of people, and they have just arrived at Xifeng. Your parents are just few miles away.' I finally found my family.

My brother Philip had been on his way to Kaiyang to the south, and our family was going to Tongzi, to the north. If he hadn't bumped into Deputy Gong's team, we would have lost this brother forever. In those days, there were no phones, emails, or texts!

It was better to be a dog in peace than a person in wartime.

Gong was the Captain of the special agent team that escorted Yang Hucheng (the general who started the Xi'an Incident with Zhang Xueliang) to Chongqing, while my father was holding Zhang Xueliang at Xifeng. They passed by each other on their way north. That was big man's business; let me talk about some of the small people.

CARRIER AND BUDDHIST NUN

I followed my father's brigade and Zhang Xueliang, and we fled from Xifeng to Tongzi, Guizhou, and stopped. All the way, not much happened, except a small episode:

a nun who fled married a bearer in our team. In a few words, she promised her life to him, the nun went up to the truck, the bearers were happy, and my father did not say anything. There were six bearers in the secret service team. Hunan farmers had nothing to do in winter. They came out to work and lifted the sedans. And they never went back their hometowns. The nun had no way to live out of the temple. Two little people needed each other, the nun got married and had food to eat, and the bearer would be a happy married man! What a happy sign!

I made a short song:

有歌為証
去年怪事少，今年怪事多。
板凳爬上了牆， 饅頭打破了鍋。

"There were few strange things last year,
and there are many strange things this year.
The bench climbed the wall,
the steamed buns broke the pot."

Chapter Twelve

TONGZI, GUIZHOU:
OCTOBER 1945 – 1946

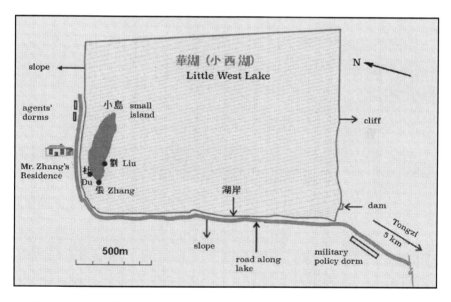

Figure 12 Map of Little West Lake near Tongzi and Zhang Xueliang's residence

Tongzi is a city between Guiyang and Chongqing (approximately 100 miles from Guiyang and 120 miles from

Chongqing). At Tongzi, there is a cave called Tianmen Cave not far from the city, caused by erosion of the river. The slope of the river near the area was very steep, and the large drop in a short distance was excellent for developing hydro power.

The 41st Arsenal of the Nationalist Army built a dam on the upper reaches of Tianmen Cave and a small hydro-power plant. The power was exclusively for the use of the arsenal and not available to Tongzi. The lake behind the dam was called Little West Lake (小西湖). There was a western style house built for the Director of the Arsenal. Dai Li liked the exclusive location, beautiful scenery, good fishing, and the availability of electric lights. It would be the perfect residence for Zhang Xueliang.

He called the director Major General Liu Shouyu (劉守愚) and borrowed his house at the lakeside for Zhang Xueliang. He also asked the military engineers to build some houses for other people to live.

Zhang Xueliang's residence sat on a platform beside Little West Lake. On the front slope there was a bamboo forest, but without obscuring the eyeline, one could see the cliffs and distant mountains on the other side of the lake. It was a ready-made landscape painting.

Zhang Xueliang's residence consisted of two separate units. The main one had five rooms on the left side. Mr. Zhang, Miss Four, Du Fa, and Wu Ma lived there, but the dining room and the kitchen were for common use for my father or our family if we were there. There was one unit with two rooms on the right side separated by a two-meter walkway, where my father worked and slept.

The best thing was there were electric lights, although there was no running water or flush toilets.

Mr. Zhang really enjoyed fishing in Tongzi. There was a small island in Little West Lake. My father and Mr. Zhang went there to fish twice a day. In the morning, they fished from nine a.m. to noon. They went back for lunch and so Mr. Zhang could take a nap, and they went back to fish from three p.m. to five p.m. or later. They crossed the fifty-meter channel by a large wooden boat, pushed by a Hunan carrier with a long bamboo pole.

The place for each man to fish was fixed. Zhang Xueliang, my father, and Du Fa each had a designated spot. Zhang Xueliang's place was at the tip of the island. He had a hut with a canopy, a canvas chair, and he used an American fishing rod.

My father's fishing spot had a smaller hut, on the left side of the island with a canopy, a canvas chair, and he use a "running" pole made of bamboo—a hand-made fishing rod with a reel.

His bodyguard Du Fa's place was close to Zhang Xueliang on his right. Du sat on a canvas stool that could be folded up. He used a homemade fishing pole, a long bamboo pole with fishing line on the tip. He was Zhang Xueliang's bodyguard, but he fished in the meantime. On the island, there were two special agents who didn't fish.

I still remember that Wu Ma once tried to fish at Du Fa's place as a guest, and she actually caught a big fish. The fish somehow got off the hook and jumped on the shore. Wu Ma laid down on top of the fish in her long dress and called loudly "Help! Help!" ("救命! 救命!"). She always wore long dresses and walked like a penguin. She was really an old-fashioned lady. I still laugh about this memory today.

They fished for carp. In the mornings, my two brothers

and I would go to the lake and throw in a fish cage. We would catch carp that way. At lunch, we'd have carp and another dish.

Figure 13 Wu Ma, Miss Four's personal maid

The bait was made by the Hunan carrier with the nickname Tall Guy (長子, or "long one"). He made a "dry dough" (枯吧) bait every day. He used leftover scallions and vegetable oil to make a dough and mixed it with wet flour and rolled it into one-centimeter balls.

He proudly distributed a bag of the bait to everyone each morning. It would be more than enough for a day's fishing.

At the end of the day, Zhang Xueliang and my father threw the extra bait into their fishing ponds, to create their own new feeding ground (養窩子 or "raise a nest").

They could catch several fish every time. They kept one or two for dinner and threw the remaining in their own ponds. Zhang Xueliang had a 2 x 4-meter pond, and there was a gate to separate it from the rice field. My father had a one-meter round pond at the corner of the rice field. They didn't pay rent for it.

Director Liu Shouyu, as the host of the place, came to fish with Zhang Xueliang, as a courtesy visit. I know the feeling of the sudden pull when a fish bites. It's so strange and unforgettable that Director Liu must have felt it. And after the first visit, he came back several times, to go fishing!

Look at the Scenery Every Day

The best scenic spot in Tongzi was Tianmen Cave and Little West, the small dam at the entrance of Little West Lake. The military police had a checkpoint there, with guards twenty-four hours a day, and no visitors were allowed.

Mr. Zhang lived there and watched the beautiful mountain and lake every day. At that time, my father had only one quarter-ton Jeep, and one truck for going to the city to buy food. It was also there for an emergency if we had to take Zhang Xueliang to escape if necessary. There was no transportation for Mr. Zhang to go out sightseeing.

For nearly two years, Zhang Xueliang rarely left his lake.

The idleness was too much to endure for those Hunan bearers. They had to do something. So, on their own, they went to the islands to grow vegetables. When we arrived, the island was a bare land. Then under the Hunan farmers' hands, it changed into a green island!

It turned out Tall Guy (長子) grew long string beans (長虹豆). The short and strong Little Wang grew cabbage. The big and strong Big Wang grew radishes. It was like each kind of man raised a different kind of dog. Their boundaries were very clearly defined, so they had no border disputes.

They sold their vegetables to the main kitchen (大廚房). The food for Mr. Zhang's kitchen (the small kitchen, or 小廚房) was bought by Hunan bearer Tan Jiayi (譚家易) every day from the city. Chicken, duck, and meat (no fish!), vegetables, and fruits. The truck could only get to the barracks. Tan Jiayi carried it on his shoulder to the small kitchen. And he would stay there, not going back to his home.

Tan, his Hunan wife, and an eleven-year-old daughter lived in a private house near the barracks.

Before dinner, Mr. Zhang always stood on the platform in front of his house, looking out to the lake and mountains.

Every day at five o'clock from the lake, a sound from the sky traveled over lake: "You, the dead ghost! Come back to eat!" Or the wife would call Tan's name. One day after five o'clock, Zhang said, "Why didn't she call today?"

CURSING THE CHINESE

One of the phrases that Zhang Xueliang often said in Tongzi is, "These Chinese!" (這些中國人!) Anyone who did not follow the rules of the New Life Movement, such as spitting, or when he read a newspaper reporting a dogfight, he would resentfully say "These Chinese!"

He would also say, "Hate that iron won't become steel" (恨鉄不成鋼), which was like a father cursing a son for not being good enough. He thought Chinese people could do better and improve themselves but didn't.

After he arrived in Taiwan, I did not hear him say this anymore. Did give up on his son?

Chapter Thirteen

GRANDFATHER LONG YINTAN

One day, we received information that our maternal grand-father had passed away in Hunan. My mother set up a place to worship her father. It was in the forest on the left bank of the Lake. We knelt on the earth and worshipped in the direction of Hunan.

Mr. Zhang and Miss Four also went with us. After we stood up, they stood at our place and bowed toward Hunan. It was a moment when we felt close, after all these years together.

I remember I saw a little wild orchid under the tree on our way back.

In the photo, Grandfather Long Yintan (龍吟譚) sat in the center. My father is the one wearing a uniform, by his side is my mother, the child is my big brother Liu Bohan (劉伯涵), and the one on left is my mother's older brother.

My grandfather died at the age of seventy-three. In my memory, he mostly lived in a rural area in Xiangyin, Hunan

(湖南湘陰) in a large house on a small hill. Grandfather's father, Long Jingsong (龍景松), served as the admiral of the Qing Dynasty. My grandfather used to be the head of the civil affairs department of Jiangxi Province, kind of like a mayor.

Figure 14 Grandfather Long Yintan (seated); l to r:
Mother's brother, Father, Mother, big brother Bohan

After he retired, my grandfather engaged in calligraphy, engraved seals, and collected antiques. He was very respected by everybody. He liked to use a small wooden bowl to crush peanuts for me and watch while I ate. I was four or five years old at the time.

My mother grew up in a scholarly family (書香世家). My mother had an open mind. After graduating from high school, she went to Nanchang Central Party School. She went to participate in building the new China. Fortunately for us, my mother met my father, her instructor in a class about politics, and they later married.

When I was four or five years old, our mother took myself and my two brothers to live with grandfather in Hunan for several months. My grandfather's study had a row of wooden cabinets with a lot of bottles filled with candy. He always took a nap on the loungers there every day. I would wait for him to fall asleep, then put my finger through the hole in the back of his chair to poke him. My grandfather would wake up, laughing loudly. I would yell, "Brothers, come eat candy!"

When my eldest brother was eight or nine years old, he was very difficult to control, so mother sent him to grandfather to educate him. After two or three years, my big brother could write very neatly and paint pretty good paintings.

Figure 15 Liu Yiguan and maternal grandfather
Long Yintan

After the Japanese occupied Changsha in 1945, my grandfather sent his grandson Long Xuexiang (龍雪詳) (twelve years old) and my big brother with a relative, Li Dahe (李達和), each carrying a bag to walk 400 hundred miles to Tongzi, to find us.

Before this, the Japanese soldiers came to Grandfather's home. He had sent his family to the mountain. He was sitting behind the desk. Two Japanese soldiers came in with guns. They saw an elegant old gentleman with a long beard sitting behind the desk in a room full of books. They looked around and took two jade stamps from the table, rubbed them twice on the face, bowed to grandfather, and left! In other homes, they took everything.

Chapter Fourteen

DARKNESS BEFORE DAWN

In 1945, shortly after arriving at Tianmen Cave, Mother took us six children to live in Tongzi City. The rented house was next door to the city hall. I was in elementary school in Tongzi. The Anti-Japanese War had reached a critical moment.

Materials for livelihood were very scarce. The value of the currency depreciated quickly. The currency that was used at the time, Fabi (法幣), was not worth the paper it was printed on; counting the money was not by piece, but by the bundle. We had to pay the tuition fees by piling up bundles of money on a rickshaw and taking it to school. Later, the school would only take rice or soybeans as payment.

In fact, we all knew that we couldn't keep the money that would depreciate so fast. Our smart mother collected all us kids' money from New Year's that included the New Year's gift money (壓歲錢) from Zhang Xueliang and the winnings from gambling with Mr. Zhang and exchanged them for three barrels of soybeans.

Every year, Mr. Zhang gave us money, and my feeling was, "I am rich," because it was a lot compared with our allowance of a few copper coins.

When I was happy, it meant, "I am happy!" Happy is a feeling at that moment, and it is a feeling that I have now. I no longer have to think that all I have is one barrel of soybeans!

At the Tongzi Primary School where I went to school, the playground was often borrowed by the Nationalist Army wounded soldiers who had retreated from the front line.

One day, I saw thirty or forty soldiers together. The seventeen- and eighteen-year-old recruits sat on the ground without guns. Seven or eight veterans, in their early twenties,[8] each stood with a rifle as a guard, to prevent them from escaping.

Those who were guarded would be our new strength to fight the Japanese soldiers. How could we win?

The wounded soldiers would get their salary on the playground. An officer would stand on a table tennis table and pass out money. After the soldiers received the money, they rushed out. They all went to the Main Street to buy a bowl of noodle or something.

The wounded soldiers always crowded the only Main Street because they had nothing to do. I liked to go there to watch a "diorama" (a box showing slides). One time, one of the wounded soldiers picked my pocket of all my 4000 yuan,

8. During the Anti-Japanese War, the recruits were enlisted at the age of fifteen or sixteen. In the next ten years, they were often killed or seriously injured. They were few veterans over the age of thirty.

all my New Year's money from Mr. Zhang. That was a lot of money. I could buy bowl of yangchun noodles (陽春麵) for ten yuan at the street corner. Why did I keep all my money in my pocket? I still can't figure that out today!

But I remember what my thought then was, "Okay, this guy could eat a few hundred bowls of noodles this coming year."

TRANSPORTATION

In the late period of the Anti-Japanese War, private trucks could not get gasoline. Some could use alcohol, but most of the trucks had been converted to burn charcoal.

The speed of charcoal vehicles was about fifteen kilometers per hour. Driving every twenty kilometers, they had to stop to reload the charcoal. When going uphill, occasionally they had to stop, the assistant had to go down and put out two wooden triangles to block the rear wheels, and then the truck could rush forward again. The assistant could climb back up into the truck by walking fast.

Guizhou is mountainous, with its famous seventy-two turns at Lou Mountain Pass (婁山關七十二枴 72). Traveling through this pass was very slow.

If someone could afford to travel, the only way was to take these trucks. It was called "catch the yellow fish" (搭黃魚), meaning one had to pay one ounce of gold to go from Chongqing to Tongzi.

The drivers became the rich bosses of the road. In each place they spent the night, they would sleep at their mistresses' places and have warm food. By the way, other drivers also shared the same "mistress" the next day.

There were two kinds of trucks at that time. One was a kind with a closed cargo cabin behind, and the rear door was locked from the outside when driving. The guests and the goods were locked inside. I rode once, and when I needed to pee, I just had to hold it.

The other was open at the back, with rails about one meter high on the left and right sides. In order to load more goods, they added a wooden bench to the three railings. The whole truck was more than three meters high, and the goods were piled up to the top. The riders had to sit on top of the goods and grab the ropes that tied the goods together. The road from Chongqing to Guiyang passed through Tongzi, and the trucks had to pass through the two gates at the north and south. We lived near the south gate. I saw how they passed through it. The clearing of the gate was less than two meters, so how could a truck of three meters high go through it? They dug into the roadbed! The smart drivers dug the gravel road down. The surface of the road became a ditch covered in black oil that leaked from these trucks struggling through over the years.

Chapter Fifteen

JOINT ANTI-JAPANESE WAR

Zhang Xueliang's Xi'an Incident prompted the second co-operation between the Guomindang and the Communist Party in 1937, who united to fight the Japanese (the first time they cooperated was when the war against the Japanese first started).

They agreed to separately fight the war each in their own way.

Both sides fought for eight years.

In July 1937, Chiang Kai-shek declared war on Japan. The Nationalist army fought a regular war on the front facing the Japanese. The Communist Party fought a guerrilla war behind the enemy.

REGULAR WAR

The regular war was led by Chiang Kai-shek and the Guomindang party.

The first major battle was the Battle at Shanghai (淞滬 會戰), from August to November 1937 for three months.

The Nationalist army had 700,000 soldiers, including the nine divisions trained by a German Supreme military adviser. The Japanese had 200,000 soldiers.

Chinese soldiers fought a furious battle at the front lines and retreated to cities in the back lines. We lost 190,000 soldiers but killed and wounded 40,000 Japanese soldiers. Every five Chinese soldiers took one Japanese with them.

That was a real surprise for Japan. They believed they would conquer China in three months!

Following that, we lost the capital Nanjing, but we fought another major battle. The Battle of Wuhan (武漢會 戰) was a furious battle that resulted in more deaths and injuries among the Chinese, as well as the Japanese soldiers.

We lost most of our fighting force including the 90,000+ German-trained soldiers in two battles. Afterward, Chiang Kai-shek had to recruit new soldiers.

These two battles were fought for two purposes: (1) To show Japan that Chinese soldiers could fight and were willing to die for their country, and to break their dream of conquering China in three months, and (2) To show Western powers, including America, that the Chinese could fight and were willing to die for their country, so the West would come to help in the future.

Chiang Kai-shek changed his long-term strategy: to fight a protracted war, on the low mountains and hills of the west and south China.

On the Central China plain, the advance of the Japanese depended on how fast the Japanese soldiers could walk. The Japanese had their tanks drive in front and their soldiers walked behind. If the soldiers could walk

100 kilometers a day, that was how far they could occupy.

Chiang Kai-shek wanted to slow them down. He led the Japanese army to the southwest, using terrain to slow down their tanks, where their cannons couldn't shoot far.

Chiang Kai-shek's long-term strategy for the war was: "Trade Space for Time" (以空間換時間) to gain time for the world to change to our advantage, such as having the Russians or the Americans come to help.

But the space was not free — it was our blood!

One inch of blood for one inch of the kingdom's lands! (一寸山河一寸血!)

Only the Chinese could do this.

China had 4.4 million square miles, and about 450 million people (before the war).

The new recruited soldiers were weak. They didn't have much to eat, had no training, and few guns (one company of 100 soldiers had seven rifles), but they were Chinese. They were willing to die for the country; they never surrendered!

The Japanese advance slowed because they had to step over the bodies of the Chinese soldiers. The soldiers' job was to lay down in front of the tanks. The last seven soldiers were responsible for taking the seven rifles to retreat to the next place where the new recruits were waiting.

And a lot of young hungry farmers waited to be recruited, to die for their country.

That was how the Japanese advanced to the west end of Hunan, after four-and-a-half years from the start of the war in July 1937. Thirty million Chinese soldiers and civilians sacrificed themselves over the total eight years of the Anti-Japanese War.

United States Came to China's Aid

In May 1944, after the Chinese Expeditionary Force rebuilt the Sino-Indian Highway, the United States used ten-wheel trucks to transport strategic materials to China. They transported them directly from India to the front line of China via Myanmar. These trucks had to go through Tongzi to get to the front line.

I remember we always went to the Main Street to watch the fleet drive through. We stretched our arms to the driver, with our thumb pointing up, and shouted, "The Best! The Best!" (頂好！頂好！) The big American drivers in uniform would stretch their arms back, with their thumbs pointed up and shouted back at us.

One strange thing is that if the driver was a Chinese-American, he would drive through without any expression. Why?

We noticed that the Americans ate corn with butter, and we also liked the red beads in the taillights of the ten-wheel trucks. We stole them and played with them like marbles, as they were red and perfectly round. Our local marbles were muddy green, and not even round.

Japanese Surrender

One day, our father took us brothers on a walk by the lake. He picked up some seeds from the roadside and threw it to us, and said, "Here is the atomic bomb!"

On August 6, 1945, the United States dropped the first atomic bomb in Hiroshima, Japan. Three days later, it dropped a second one in Nagasaki. Six days later, Emperor

Hirohito announced Japan's unconditional surrender. It was August 15, 1945.

The Anti-Japanese War had ended. Did China win? No!

China didn't win the war by itself. Chiang Kai-shek didn't surrender; the Chinese never surrendered to any foreign forces. The only exceptions were Mongolia and Manchuria; they conquered China, but later they became Chinese.

RETURN HOME

After the victory of the Anti-Japanese War, all the service people were sent home with extra money paid by the Military Bureau.

The chefs, waiters, drivers, and Hunan bearers were all sent back. Most of them returned by riding the three-meters-tall trucks mentioned before, but they did not have to pay gold. The agents escorted them to the trucks and put them on it.

When we were sent to Taiwan in late 1946, one of the most distressing things was that my father's adjutant couldn't take his family to Taiwan with us. Only our family could go to Taiwan first. The other agents' families had to go back to their native homes first and wait for their husbands to pick them up after we settled down in Taiwan.[9] The adjutant's wife and three kids had to return to their hometown in Hunan first. They sat on the pile of goods and tied themselves to ropes.

---

9 . A lot of the agents never sent for their families, many of them married again in Taiwan.

But when the truck made a sharp turn, a newborn baby was thrown out the truck, flew to the roadside and died! How could a mother not hold tight to her baby? When she rushed to reach out and grab the two-year-old and three-year-old sons sitting on both sides of her to prevent them from being thrown out, her hands that held the baby were released, and he flew away from his mother!

Writing this, I cried. My wife said to me, "It's too tragic, don't write it." But I still wrote it down. This is one of the countless tragedies behind the Anti-Japanese War. This little baby should not have been sacrificed in vain.

Those type of horrible things happened during the war.

Chapter Sixteen

THE COMMUNISTS FIGHT THE JAPANESE: MARCH OF THE VOLUNTEERS

"Stand up! We don't want to be slaves!
Use our blood and body, build our new
Great Wall."

The slogan of the Communist Party was not just a sentence. It was what really happened.

The first sentence woke up how many souls?

That sorrowful song was clearer and easier to remember than Chiang Kai-shek's declaration of war.

The volunteers marched into history and changed history!

The song was sung loudly.

The Communists engaged in guerrilla warfare against the Japanese. In 1937, the Eighth Route Army and the New Fourth Army (八路軍和新四軍) of the Communist Army had only 50,000 soldiers. They used flexible guerrilla warfare in the enemy-occupied area. They assaulted, killed and ran, making the Japanese army worry all the time. They lost few soldiers, and in the meantime, they recruited farmers and workers to join their force.

By July 1940, the Communists had grown to more than 400,000 soldiers, and they had an anti-Japanese base area of 100 million people and an organization of two million militia.

At the end of 1943, the Japanese army was seriously underpowered, because they sent most of their soldiers to the Pacific War against the American army. They had to relocate their forces to occupied cities and stopped attacking the guerrilla warfare base.

From the beginning of 1944 to 1945, the Communist Party led the guerrillas and militia and began to counter-attack the Japanese Army and the Puppet Army (the army of the puppet government of Wang Jingwen that obeyed Japanese command in Manchuria, with a maximum of one million soldiers). The Puppet Army didn't resist the Communists because they were Chinese. The Communists slowed down the main force of the Japanese army, so that the Japanese army was trapped in the big cities and the main roads. They couldn't attack the Nationalist troops on the main frontline.

After eight years of fighting, the Japanese army killed a lot of soldiers. By 1944, there were still one million soldiers. That was because the Communist Party was expanding while fighting.

China is a country of agriculture. Before the 1920s, landlords oppressed tenant farmers. After the May Thirtieth Movement (五卅惨案) (where British officers shot and killed thirteen Chinese protestors against imperialism in Shanghai), the Chinese Communist Party organized a strike in Shanghai. The more than 200,000 workers organized by Liu Shaoqi (劉少奇) and other leaders set up the Shanghai Federation of Trade Unions, launched more than 200,000 workers to strike, and 50,000 students went on strike. Most businessmen took part in the strike. The Communist Party that had fought for the peasants also fought for the workers and started to organize the people.

They promised that tenant farmers would get the fields they tilled and that workers would no longer be exploited by their bosses. Naturally, they tended to join the Communist Party. The young would join the army. When the country was in hardship, the students were the most enthusiastic and patriotic and were the first to join the fight.

Therefore, the more the Communist guerrillas fought, the more people joined them. In 1937, they had 50,000 guerrillas, and after fighting for eight years, they had one million soldiers.

ALL CHINESE ANTI-JAPANESE WAR

In the first four-and-a-half years of the Anti-Japanese War, China was divided into the Nationalist-controlled area and the enemy-occupied area. The Northwest, north China, central China, and southern China (except Xiangnan, 湘南) were all occupied by the Japanese. These were resource abundant and rich farmlands with rivers and lakes filled with fish. Plus, Japan controlled the coastline with all of China's industry as well as commerce along the coast.

What did the Nationalist-controlled area have?

The Nationalist-controlled areas were hills and mountains, except the Sichuan basin. The Sichuan basin contained farmlands producing rice, large natural gas reserves, and rich mining resources. The rock salt produced there was the only source of salt for all the Nationalist-controlled area.

All other places were poor. Materials were extremely scarce, and the people relied on smuggling to obtain supplies for their livelihoods. Military strategic materials also had to be smuggled from the enemy-occupied areas.

The Nationalist-controlled poor half of China couldn't fight the occupied rich half of China. We needed to use all of China's manpower and resources to fight the Japanese. How could we do this?

General Dai Li had three strategies: (1) print counterfeit banknotes, (2) smuggle products, and (3) sell opium. These strategies were approved by Chiang Kai-shek, and the Nationalist Government agreed and participated in them.

The operation was carried out by Dai Li's Military Control Bureau and its peripheral organizations. A Wartime Freight Bureau (戰時貨運局) was set up under the Executive Yuan (the National Treasury) under Dai Li's control. Dai Li became the Head of the Anti-Smuggling Department (緝私署) under the Ministry of Finance.

1. Printing and Counterfeiting

The occupied area used the currency printed by Wang Jingwei's government (Wang currency). Dai Li counterfeited it at a large scale at Chongqing and shipped it to the occupied area. Dai Li bought the most advanced copperplate printing machine and a large amount of printing paper from the United States. He also paid a high salary to Mr. Olmer, a counterfeit manufacturing expert from the United States, to oversee the operation at one of the

Military Bureau bases, at Yangjia Mountain, Chongqing (重慶楊家山).

The printed counterfeit banknotes (Wang currency) were transported to Shanghai by the Military Bureau's pipeline and handed over to Du Yuesheng (杜月笙), a mob boss in Shanghai, to buy gold, cotton yarn, and other strategic materials in the black market. There were two advantages to doing this. One, most of the gold went to the Executive Yuan. Some of it went to Dai Li for his operations. The war supplies were smuggled by Dai Li and handed over to the military.

Second, a large number of fake counterfeit banknotes flooded the market of the occupied area. The Wang currency depreciated accordingly. The loss of purchase power of the people was the same as if they paid taxes to Wang Jingwei's government, but the benefits actually went to Dai Li. Most were used for the Anti-Japanese War.

2. Smuggling of Goods

The area that was Nationalist occupied was very poor, materials were extremely scarce, and the people relied on smuggling to obtain supplies for their livelihood. There were small groups of professional smugglers that smuggled in life support goods from the occupied areas and smuggled out mainly opium. They were selfish and greedy criminals who had to be arrested and their goods confiscated. This was the duty of the Anti-Smuggling Department, of which Dai Li was the Department head, and they did a very thorough job. The bad guys were put in jail, and the opium was confiscated.

Military strategic materials also were smuggled from the enemy-occupied areas. The partisan guerilla forces of

10,000 people under the control of Dai Li could do it easily. The transportation was done by the Wartime Freight Bureau under the control of Dai Li.

The goods smuggled in were gold, cotton yarn, and other strategic materials brought in the black market in Shanghai. Plus, they included goods confiscated from the criminal smugglers. The goods smuggled out were prepared by Dai Li's Military Control Bureau, mainly opium and some metals, plus items confiscated from the bad guys, mainly opium.

3. SELLING OPIUM

From 1941-1944, our family lived in Kaiyang County, Guizhou, in front of the city hall. At the time, a lot of people smoked opium in Guizhou. The government carried out a policy to ban opium. I saw them burn the smoking equipment several times, piling up a big pile of smoking pipes on the city hall front courtyard, and burned it while a lot of people watched. But they never burned the opium, saving it for smuggling purposes.

At that time, many people all over China smoked opium. Chiang Kai-shek pushed his policy to ban opium in the provinces under his control, and they burned a lot of smoking pipes and saved a lot of opium.

That opium eventually fell into Dai Li's hands, and it was smuggled out to sell it to Chinese in occupied areas. Mostly via Du Yuesheng, the mob boss in Shanghai. In addition, Chief Executive Kong Xiangxi (孔詳熙) collected hundreds of thousands of kilograms of opium from Sichuan provinces and sold them to Du Yuesheng in Shanghai. And Dai Li smuggled those from Shanghai through the occupied area to Hong Kong and other overseas areas. The profits were divided between Du Yuesheng and Dai Li.

The Executive Yuan received most of the money from the smokers at home and abroad in China. They spent that on the Anti- Japanese War. But the money came from the Chinese who smoked opium smuggled to them by Dai Li.

The health of the smokers was destroyed. They sacrificed their health to save the country. What is the red line? Who could draw the red line? Is the red line different at a different time?

Where would you draw the red line?

I would draw my red line for that time as follows:

The Chinese would never surrender to Japan!
Chinese lives did not matter! China mattered!
This was the All-Chinese Anti-Japanese War.

Chapter Seventeen

Here is what my brother Philip wrote:

> Recalling the victory of the Anti-Japanese War (1945), my father talked to us while we walked together. My father said that he received instructions from above to ask Zhang Xueliang to write to his former subordinate generals in the Northeast army, to persuade them to come back to Chiang Kai-shek's side. At that time, the Northeastern army was mostly in the northeast, serving under the puppet state of Manchuria.
>
> Zhang Xueliang wrote several letters to his generals. I only remember that Zhang Xuesi (張學思, a brother of Zhang Xueliang) was one of them.
>
> It was rumored that the Communist Party tried to force the Northeast generals Lu Zhengcao (呂正操) and Li Yunchang (李運昌) to help them

to accept the surrender of the Japanese Army in Manchuria to China. That may be misinformation, because they (Lu Zhengcao and Li Yunchang) already served under the puppet state of Manchuria.

As far as I know, Yang Hucheng (the other general who started the Xi'an Incident with Zhang Xueliang) was indeed under house arrest at the base of the Chongqing Military Command of the Sino-U.S. Cooperation Institute. The person in charge was Gong Guoyan (龔國彥), the former deputy under my father, when they served as the guard team of Zhang Xueliang. Yang Hucheng was in house arrest accompanied by his wife and a daughter (only six or seven years old at the time). A special medical officer took care of them. They had no freedom, but he had nothing to do with the Xi'an Incident.

I was in Qinghua Middle School in Chongqing. During summer vacation, I saw Gong Guoyan and his wife, but I never saw Yang Hucheng or his wife. I only heard that Yang tried to commit suicide by swallowing gold but was fine after the rescue.

Later, I heard that on the eve of the Mainland's loss to the Communist Party, Yang, his wife and the little girl were shot together.

What I heard was that, in 1945, when the Military Control Bureau prepared to retreat to Taiwan, Yang Hucheng, his wife, as well the six-year-old daughter were killed with long knives! The special medical officer with them was shot as well.

The way the Military Bureau punished people was as follows: No trial was needed; what the Chief of the Bureau said counted. The punishment could be ranked as:

1. Killed with long knife (example: Yang Hucheng and his family);
2. Individually shot with a handgun, buried in a single grave (example: the special medical officer with Yang Hucheng and Zhang Xueliang's bodyguard Li);
3. Lined up and shot with rifles, buried in mass graves (example: the students suspected to be Communists in the Bureau's jail in 1945 before the Bureau's retreat to Taiwan);
4. Shot with light machine gun (the remaining people jailed or in the concentration camps at that time); and
5. Put in jail (I don't know what happened to some of the special agents that my father put in jail).

The war years in China were very difficult. I think about all the ways so many Chinese people lost their lives: fighting for what they believed in (whether Nationalists or Communists fighting each other or against the Japanese); being loyal to, associated with, or being a family member of a losing side; or from being in the wrong place at the wrong time (like the accidents).

Chapter Eighteen

MO DEHUI VISITS

On April 22, 1946, the President of the Examination Department Mo Dehui (莫德惠), a delegate to the National Assembly and one of the most respected persons of Northwest, visited Zhang Xueliang at Tianmen Cave, Tongzi. As a special envoy sent by Chiang Kai-shek, Mo stayed for five days.

When he was there, Mo Dehui told Zhang Xueliang:

1. Friends in the Northeast always greeted Zhang Xueliang. In other words, if he would come out to lead, they would all listen to him.
2. He told him the "true news" of the Northeast (the situation in the Northeast).
3. The Soviet Union invaded the Northeast on August 9, 1945, and occupied many cities, confiscated the weapons of the 700,000-strong Japanese Army, and gave these weapons to the Communist Army there.

When Mo Dehui talked with Zhang Xueliang, my father was mostly present. What did they talk about?

At the beginning of April 1946, after the Soviet Union withdrew from the Northeast, the Red Army and the Nationalist Army each tried to occupy the land and take control in the Northeast. The Communists grabbed the country land and the small towns. The Nationalist Army grabbed the big city. Although the Nationalist Army was dominant at that time, Chiang Kai-shek knew to control the whole Northeast was not a sure thing.

Mo Dehui proposed a plan that would have allowed Zhang Xueliang to leave his house arrest temporarily to help the country. He came up with the following strategies to send Zhang Xueliang to the Northeast to recover the Northeast for Chiang Kai-shek:

1. Zhang Xueliang could become a special commissioner and be put in charge of politics.
2. He could also send three-star general Bai Chongxi (白崇禧) as the deputy and put him in charge of the military.
3. He would send Chiang's son, Jiang Jingguo (蔣經國), as the special commissioner of the Ministry of Foreign Affairs.

Zhang Xueliang was a wise man. When he heard about the plan, he knew that Chiang Kai-shek wanted to use his prestige to recruit his previous subordinates in the Northeast, Lü Zhengcao (呂正操) and others, as well as his younger brother Zhang Xuesi to re-establish control over the guerrilla organizations of the Northeast.

The army was commanded by Bai Chongxi, with Jiang

Jingguo secretly watching the bottom line for Chiang Kai-shek. Zhang Xueliang would have been only a useful puppet. If Zhang Xueliang was willing to be a puppet, he would already have been the Emperor of Manchuria.[10]

After ten years of house arrest, Zhang Xueliang had not lost his pride. He did not choose to go back to the good days, but instead chose the American fishing rod that Chiang Kai-shek sent to him.

Zhang Xueliang continued fishing, and Chiang Kai-shek lost the Northeast, and then lost mainland China.

---

10. In the September 18th Incident of 1931, after the Japanese army occupied the Northeast, it was established as Manchuria. Japan asked Zhang Xueliang to be the Emperor, but Zhang did not accept. He said, "I am Chinese."

Chapter Nineteen

CHONGQING, SICHUAN:
OCTOBER 15 - DECEMBER 2, 1946

DAI MANSION

Chiang Kai-shek finally asked Zhang Xueliang to leave Guizhou. They planned to go to Chongqing to wait for the plane to take him to Taiwan. On October 15, 1946, at four o'clock in the morning, the retinue left Tongzi Tianmen Cave. The car was sent by Chongqing. This time, it was still protected by the original special agents and the military police company. The team was led by a three-quarter-ton medium-sized Jeep. The main team was led by a quarter-ton small Jeep, the adjutant Zhao Xianrui (趙顯瑞) was riding in it.

Mr. Zhang, Miss Four, and my parents followed the small Jeep in a sedan. We children, Du Fa, and Wu Ma sat in a full-size Jeep. The other special agents and military police, riding on several ten-wheeled trucks, followed behind.

I remembered that Du Fa brought a large bag of oranges very cheaply at a village along the road in Guizhou. He opened one, and it was filled with worms. I remembered those children each holding up a bag of oranges running after our jeep; the fastest one sold his bag. Later, we learned from the next village that the village we had passed was the only one with the wormy oranges. The wonders of nature!

When we approached the ferry crossing in the afternoon, there was a large military truck in front of the road deliberately driving in the middle of the road to prevent others from overtaking it. He wanted to be the first to get on the ferry boat. Zhao Xianrui ordered his small Jeep to pass the truck from the shoulder (the Jeep almost turned over) and pointed a gun at the driver. When he stopped, the machine gunman Zhang Fucheng (張富成) took his light machine gun and hit the driver with the butt. The assistant rushed to the back and saluted my father, wearing his one-star general uniform standing outside the car.

My father said loudly, "Don't beat him, don't beat him!"

The military police sitting on the big truck only watched with enthusiasm. In fact, the driver did not know that our first traffic guard had arrived at the ferry early, and the ferry was seized waiting for us to board.

At six o'clock in the afternoon, we arrived at Songling Hill, Gele Mountain, in Chongqing. (重慶歌樂山松林坡). We stayed in a house with screen doors, electric lights, and flush toilets. It was one of the three residences of Dai Li in Chongqing.

The house was very big. Mr. Zhang, Miss Four and their servants, and my parents with my younger siblings lived there. I stayed with seven or eight special agents in a long room with eight or nine canvas beds. I slept in the middle.

One day, when Zhang Xueliang and some guests were eating dinner, Wang Shizhong (王世忠) (the "Duck Captain"),[11] who was twelve, rushed in and shouted to my mother, "Mrs. Liu, Mrs. Liu! I couldn't lift the toilet!" He had tried to pick up the flush toilet to empty it. Everyone at the dinner table laughed loudly, and some sprayed rice from their mouths!

After Zhang Xueliang arrived in Chongqing, the director of the Intelligence Bureau, Mao Renfeng did not come to see him. He sent the Deputy director Zhang Yanfo (張嚴佛), a two-star general who outranked my father, to oversee the reception. Zhang Yanfo brought Xu Yuanju (徐遠舉) and other high-level special agents to see him and threw a lot of parties for him.

Zhang Yanfo oversaw strategy for the Bureau; he was very tricky and knew how to talk. We were in Chongqing to wait for the plane to go to Taiwan and lived in the Dai Mansion for a month and a half.

He told Zhang Xueliang we were waiting to fly to Nanjing (Chiang Kai-shek was the Chairman in Nanjing at that time) and told my father he wasn't allowed to tell Zhang Xueliang we were going to Taiwan until after we arrived.

When we arrived in Taiwan, my father told Zhang Xueliang that it was their destination.

That got Zhang Xueliang very mad at my father. It damaged the trust built over ten years and for the coming three years in Taiwan.

---

11. Before the Hunan bearer, Da Lao Wang, was sent back to his hometown, his son Wang Shizhong was left with my father, and the "Duck Captain" was relegated to a being a small serviceman.

It was Zhang Yanfo's strategy for himself; he wanted the job of taking care of Zhang Xueliang in Taiwan in the future.

GOODBYE TO THE MAINLAND:
NOVEMBER 2, 1946

On November 2, 1946, my father accompanied Zhang Xueliang, our family (except my older brothers, who stayed in Chongqing for high school), and a dozen special agents, and flew to Baishiyi Airport to fly to Nanchang, Hubei. We would all then fly southeast to Taiwan, arriving in Taipei Songshan Airport that afternoon.

The day before, my father had sent an able assistant, Liu Changqing (劉長清), with twenty special agents who took the same type of plane to Taiwan. They went to prepare the villa for us to live, arranged by Taiwan's Chief Executive Chen Yi (台灣行政長官陳儀).

Previously, the service people, including the driver, chef, waiter, and Hunan bearers, had already been sent back to their homes before we left Tongzi.

The military police assigned to us also returned to their headquarters after we left Chongqing. Other members of the team who had their families with us were then sent back to their hometown first, to be picked up after the men arrived in Taiwan. My family was the only one who could go together with our father.

I left the Mainland, saying goodbye to my childhood. I was thirteen years old when I left mainland China for Taiwan. The next time I would visit the Mainland again was over four decades later, after I emigrated to the United

States and was then living in Venezuela, at the age of fifty-six, in 1992.

Mr. Zhang knew my childhood the best. He described me with this eight-word comment:

"Cling to life, afraid to die. Love to eat, lazy to work." (貪生怕死,好吃懶做).

This was what the big fat man Zhang Xueliang (大胖子 張學良) said of me, the little fat boy, Liu Shoutze (小胖子 劉叔慈) when I was ten years old.

I always wanted to ask Mr. Zhang to give me two "NOTs" to change the comment into:

"Cling to life, NOT afraid to die. Love to eat, NOT lazy to work." (貪生不怕死,好吃不懶做).

However, those two words were not to be given to me by Mr. Zhang.

I have been working for them for all my life.

I cling to life and am NOT afraid to die. I love to eat and am NOT lazy to work.

I really must thank Mr. Zhang for his "encouragement."

Chapter Twenty

TO TAIWAN:
NOVEMBER 2, 1946 - JANUARY 1947

On November 2, 1946, at 6:30 in the morning, we took off from Chongqing Baishiyi Airport. At noon we arrived at Wuhan, Hubei. Zhang Xueliang thought that the next stop was Nanjing. We were sitting on the C3 transport plane. There was a row of canvas chairs on both sides of the body. The middle open space was full of Mr. Zhang's luggage.

My father also prepared a large sack of pears and a large bag of bread (dry hard bread that was baked yellow). Mr. Zhang and Miss Four sat at the front, on the left side. When the two American pilots entered, Miss Four spoke fluent English to the pilots, and Zhang Xueliang also said a few broken words in English. My parents and us four younger kids sat in front on the opposite side, and Du Fa and Wu Ma and the special agents sat in the back. We were about twenty people altogether. The other twenty secret agents had been taken to Taiwan by Liu Changqing on the same kind of plane the day before. No one ate much; only I kept eating the hard bread and pears.

Before noon, our plane arrived at Wuhan to refuel, and everyone got off the plane. Two American pilots were standing under the wing. We were on the right side of the plane. At this time, a large group of people approached our plane. They were men dressed up in suits and women wearing fashionable long qipao robes. The man leading the group was a two-star general in his full uniform. They were going to take a picture with our plane as the background.

Deputy Xiong Zhongqing walked up, followed by four special agents with their guns drawn but pointing to the ground. Deputy Xiong said in his Hubei tongue, "Don't take a picture, don't take a picture."

The two-star general shouted, "Who are you? I am the Guard commander here. I control this place!"

Deputy Xiong just said again, "Don't take a picture, don't take a picture."

When the general approached, Zhang Fucheng took the lead, and the four special agents pulled out their weapons.

The Guard commander might not have understood the Hubei tongue, but when the agents stepped one step forward waving their guns, they left without a word.

When we took off again, we flew southeast toward Taiwan. In the afternoon, we landed at Taipei Songshan Airport. The mayor of Hsinchu County, Liu Qiguang (劉啓光), and the director of the Taipei Station of the Military Control Bureau, Lin Dingli (林頂立) and Deputy Liu Guoqing (劉戈青) came to meet us.

It was at that moment that Zhang Xueliang knew he was in Taiwan. He became very angry, especially toward my father. Up until then, my father and Zhang Xueliang had a gentleman's agreement where my father would tell him where they were going each time they moved. This time, my father did not tell him because he was ordered not to.

Lin Dingli invited everyone to dinner at his house, which was a bungalow in the Danshui River Dike.

No Words

The meal was served in a big room, with two long tables. The host, Mr. Zhang, Miss Four, and my family were at one table. Mr. Zhang didn't say one word the whole time. The special agents were at another table. There was a large lobster in the middle of each table. The dishes were served one by one. After four or five courses, a bowl of water came by for washing hands before eating fruit, such as bananas and pineapples. Were we finished eating? No! This was only the first round. The main dishes were to come!

We were surprised to eat lobster because we had never seen it before. We didn't know what it was. I thought it was for decoration.

At this time, the agents' table burst into laughter. Someone was drinking the water that was supposed to be for hand washing, and someone ate a banana with the skin.

I was much more knowledgeable. I had eaten bananas in Guiyang when I was six years old. I didn't drink the bowl of water because I didn't like it. The strange thing is that Mr. Zhang didn't laugh or make any sound. It was unlike him, as he usually was the only one talking and laughing loudly at any party.

When we arrived at the hotel in Hsinchu, at dinner time, mayor Liu Qiguang hosted us for dinner. The same seating arrangements, the same big lobsters, the same dishes, and Mr. Zhang still did not say a word. The difference was that no one drank the hand washing water or ate a banana with its skin.

Later, I learned that the best banquet meal in Taiwan was the lobster meal. In addition to using the largest lobster, it was necessary to add the most expensive dishes, such as abalone, sea cucumber, and the like. It was no wonder that Hsinchu had the same dinner as did Taipei.

GENTLEMAN'S AGREEMENT

As mentioned above, Zhang Xueliang and my father had a gentleman's agreement. It wasn't written or verbal. It was a trust developed between them over the ten years, after going through many things together. They kept their own positions, respected each other, and were always honest with each other. Specifically, every time my father got an order to move, he would tell Zhang Xueliang immediately after receiving the order, so that he could mentally prepare for it.

When we came to Taiwan this time, my father knew that was the destination when they arrived in Chongqing, but he didn't tell Mr. Zhang until they arrived in Taipei.

My father was very sorry, even though it was a trick done by Zhang Yanfo, who was responsible for receiving Zhang Xueliang in Chongqing. He told Zhang Xueliang they were going to Nanjing but ordered my father to tell him about Taiwan after they arrived.

Zhang Xueliang felt deceived. My father had broken their unspoken agreement.

Zhang Xueliang didn't trust my father after that, and he held that feeling for the next year during the coming Incident of February 28, 1937. My mother got depressed and had to be hospitalized in October 1937.

Chapter Twenty-One

QINGQUAN: ISOLATED

Liu Changqing came to pick us up the first day. The first thing he told my mother was, "The people here don't wear shoes in the room." My mother asked what to wear, and he said, "wear the box" (which turned out to be slippers). Then we went to our residence in Zhudong Qingquan (竹東清泉).

My parents accompanied Mr. Zhang and Miss Four in the sedan. The other people took different cars like jeeps and trucks. First, they went to Zhudong by highway, then to Qingquan on a thirty-five-kilometer-long road used for transporting timber. The last fifteen kilometers were excavated out of the forest along the mountain. The width was only large enough for one truck. Occasionally, some dirt would be pushed out to form a terrace so that one truck could pull over to let an oncoming truck pass. The road surface was paved with earth and stone. After the soil had been eroded for a long time, there were many horizontal grooves on the road surface. It took us more than two hours to get to the Taoshan Tunnel (桃山隧道), which was excavated from rock without support or ceilings, the rocks hanging out from the roof and sticking out from the walls.

When the sedan passed the tunnel, my mother saw that the faces of Mr. Zhang and Miss Four turned blue. Zhang Xueliang was a military man; he knew that he was entering a desperate area. If the entrance was blocked, no one could get out! But then again, during the February 28 Incident, my father blocked the entrance, and no one could get in either. That saved us.

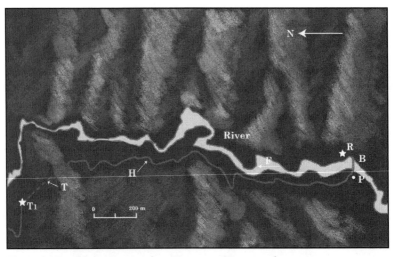

Figure 16 Road into compound at Qingquan. T1 = tunnel entrance; T = Taoshan Tunnel; H = highway; R = Zhang Xueliang's residence; B = wooden footbridge; P = police station and military barracks; F = direction of river flow

Five kilometers away, we arrived at Qingquan. The cars stopped at the left end of a wooden bridge, and everybody walked across the bridge to the residence, the villa of Prince Akihito.

The place we lived in was on the right bank of a pedestrian bridge. On a separate platform, after crossing the bridge, you could walk less than one hundred meters to the gate of a bamboo wall. There was only one small road under the cliff to reach the gate. Behind it was a very steep mountain, with a cliff on the left, with a short trail connected to a suspension bridge.

This place seemed isolated to Zhang Xueliang.

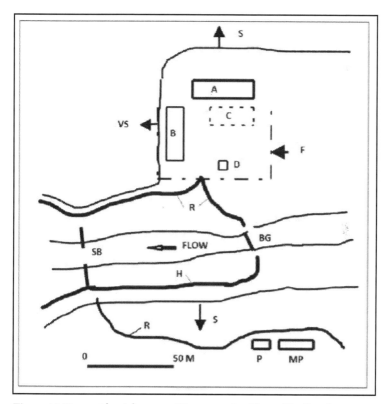

Figure 17 Our residential area at Qingquan. A = Zhang Xueliang's residence; B = special agents' dorm; C = tennis court; D = hot spring; F = bamboo wall; S = high mountain; VS = overhanging rock; R = trail; BG = wooden footbridge; H = highway; P = police station; MP = military police barracks

What about my father? For him, it was a leisurely time to study Buddhist books and meditate on the Zen.

For us, it was a paradise, I (at age thirteen, no school yet) read the "Story of the Bamboo Forest" behind the glass window of my own room. In our tatami house, there was a hallway behind the glass windows where I sat and looked at the "Pipa" tree. My sister, who was seven years old, went to school for the indigenous people (one teacher and few students), my brother Frank (the big barbarian boy 大蠻子, who was four years old), played with and assaulted snakes, and my little brother Alex (two years old), hung on my mother's arms.

Mr. Zhang's residence was a rectangular Japanese-style bungalow. It was the summer retreat villa for the Prince Akihito (the Japanese Emperor). The door was in the middle.

Figure 18 The door to the residence, l to r: Mo Dehui (□□□), Mr. Zhang

In the photo, Mr. Zhang and Miss Four are sitting in the brightest corner of their corridor. Later, Mr. Zhang put a desk there and used it as his study.

There were two wings on the left and right of the door. Each wing had five rooms of eight tatami mats,[12] paper doors, and paper windows.

A long hallway was lined with a floor-to-ceiling glass frame on the front of all the rooms.

Mr. Zhang, Miss Four, Du Fa, and Wu Ma lived in the right wing, because it had better light. Mr. Zhang's bedroom was the first room at the far right; the second room was their living room, where all the walls were lined with Mr. Zhang's string-bound books. Mr. Zhang's reading and writing was in the front of the corridor. Wu Ma lived in the third room, and Du Fa lived in the fourth.

Figure 19 Mr. Zhang and Miss Four sit in the corridor.

12. Japanese-style housing was covered with tatami mats, which were mats five centimeters thick. A standard size for a mat was 180 x 90 centimeters, which covered an area of 1.62 square meters. The common room was named with the number of the tatami mats; most were six or eight tatami rooms. Including the niche, the length and width of the rooms were about 4.5 x2.7 meters.

The fifth room was empty, and it was a guest room. After May 1948, Zhou Nianxing (周念行) lived here. He was well versed in the history of the Ming Dynasty and was sent by the Military Control Bureau to assist Zhang Xueliang in his study of Ming Dynasty history. His son Zhou Yongxun (周雍遜) told us that his father said, "Zhang Xueliang is very clever, but he didn't read much." As a result, he was sent to teach Zhang Xueliang the history of the Ming Dynasty required by Zhang Xueliang. He was with Zhang Xueliang for three years. It was as if he also lost his freedom for three years.

The left wing also had five rooms, all of which were eight tatami mats large, and they also had wide corridors and floor-to-ceiling windows. My father, mother, younger siblings, and I lived in the first three rooms.

The photo is our family portrait, sitting in the front hallway of our bedroom, about 1950. I am the first person from the left.

The other two rooms were for two agents and the maids.

Figure 20 Liu Family, back row l to r: author (Bernard), Theresa, Mother, Father, Bohan, Philip. Front row l to r: Alex, Frank (~1950)

There was a walkway and toilet in the back of the left- and right-wing rooms. It was a beautiful place, but there was no electricity, so we used gas lamps.

Our drinking water came from a mountain spring. There was a small pool in the cliff behind the staff quarters. A bamboo tube was used to get water from the pool. The water was clear and cool.

Most people sat on the mats cross-legged and did not wear shoes. They had to clean the floor every day with a damp cloth. Mr. Zhang added a double bed in his bedroom. My father slept on a bed alone in the first room. Mom and we slept on the tatami floor in the second room.

There were only about twenty special agents who flew with us from mainland China. After their arrival in Hsinchu, another twenty-some younger agents were sent to Taiwan from Chongqing.

They all lived in the barracks near the rock cliff on the left side of the gate.

The military platoon lived on the other side of the river, near the local police station.

Chapter Twenty-Two

INDIGENOUS MOUNTAIN PEOPLE

There were a lot of indigenous "mountain people" living on the hills on both sides of the Qingquan. Now they are called "original inhabitants." They were not like Han Chinese. They had narrow and concave faces. They were simple and straightforward. They hunted and planted crops suitable for the high mountains. They used gunpowder guns and long knives for hunting. They planted sweet potatoes, fruit trees, bananas, oranges, and other fruits. There was a lot of wild yam on the mountain.

The indigenous people dug up the roots, put them into a wooden trough and added some water, and two or three women each held a wooden bar to hit the slurry. Some salt would be added to the dried cake, they rounded and baked it on a stove, which turned it yellowish, and that was their major food year round. They also bought rice, and sweet potatoes made up their staple food. They would hunt for their meat. Women would weave colorful linen clothes, and older women had tattoos on their faces. They grew up in the natural environment, living on whatever they could get, eating something and buying rice wine to drink. There was no entertainment in the mountains, so the girls sang and danced and the men drank. When they were half drunk, they got up and walked left and right with a few big steps. They stepped to the beat, their bodies twisting and dancing.

They didn't deal with people from the outside, nor did they do business. They didn't bully people, and others didn't dare bully them, as the men carried three-foot long knives every day! Only the tribal chief Zhao Wanghua (趙旺華) served as the director of the police station in Qingquan. He had five or six police who were also "mountain men."

More than fifty years prior, Japanese soldiers came to Taiwan and went to the mountains to rule them. When they fought, they did not know how many Japanese soldiers who went into the barracks of the mountain people in the middle of the night were beheaded. The mountain men cut their heads off with knives and dried them and hung them around their necks as trophies. (They always carried long knives for self-defense or hunting.) An altar on the side of Mr. Zhang's residence was made by the Japanese for the Japanese soldiers.

There were also several Hakka Chinese (客家人) in Qingquan who ran grocery stores near the road at the other side of the wooden bridge, selling candy, wine, rice, and groceries. It was the place where everyone met and talked.

In the photo, the two women with scarves had tattoos on their faces. They and the two barefooted girls were all mountain people. The girl on the left is my sister, next to her is Miss Four, the second one on the right is my mother. Note that the toes of the barefooted girls were very open. That was because they walked on the mountain. The adults' feet were thicker. Their bare feet were very good for walking on the mountain; they wouldn't feel stones, wouldn't be afraid of splinters, and they wouldn't slip. It was better than any shoes!

Figure 21 My mother, sister, and Miss Four with indigenous women and children

Everyone settled down, but then the problem surfaced.

As mentioned previously, Zhang Xueliang was very angry at my father, feeling deceived when my father brought him to Taiwan without prior notice, even though he had been under orders not to tell. Zhang Xueliang lost most of his trust in my father. As a result, my father had to make special efforts to please Mr. Zhang, while keeping his position during the eleven years they lived at Qingquan.

143

GUARDING ZHANG XUELIANG

Taiwan is separated from mainland China by the South Sea, and we lived in the mountains where the environment was simple, and the terrain was hidden. The military police assigned to my father was reduced to one platoon, and there were fewer special agents. The agent guards only set up a post at the gate during the day, and only two members were placed in front of Mr. Zhang's rooms. The box gun was put away during the daytime; they only carried a small pistol on their backs under plainclothes. Zhang Xueliang couldn't see any guns, because he always walked in front, and if he was standing to talk, the agents would stand in a circle facing him, so Zhang Xueliang wouldn't see any guns.

On New Year's Day, my father would call all the agents to pay tribute to Zhang Xueliang. My father would accompany Mr. Zhang and Miss Four standing on the walkway of their room. All the agents lined up below, and the deputy led all of them to bow toward Zhang Xueliang. Mr. Zhang would bow back, but Miss Four would only bow slightly to show she only could receive a little of the honors. My father just stood there to show his respect but didn't bow to Zhang Xueliang.

Their only communication with the outside was by the police phone line. They used trucks to buy food at Zhudong Town every four days. They had to buy two large blocks of ice each time. Mr. Zhang's kitchen had a gas refrigerator; they needed to put ice in it to keep meat for four days.

My father also sent a senior agent, Zhao Xianrui (趙獻瑞) to Zhudong Town to be the eyes and ear for our team, obtain information, and to watch for unusual activities. He lived in a small house behind the district office. For the convenience of his work, he married a local woman.

My father made friends with the Mayor of Zhudong Town. Mayor Ho was a Fujian native, and all the district chiefs were from Fujian.

Chapter Twenty-Three

FEBRUARY 28 INCIDENT
(二二八事件)

UNKNOWN SITUATION

On February 28, 1947, senior agent Zhao Xianrui, the eyes and ears for our team in Zhudong Town, called to report that there was turmoil in Taipei. Mobs in the streets were beating up people from other provinces. What caused this was that a law enforcement officer from the Public Sales Bureau accidentally killed a Taiwanese woman selling illicit cigarettes on the street.

After receiving this news, my father sent Gong Wengyu (龔文玉), a Taiwanese man, to drive his truck to Zhudong to buy rice and vegetables (our buying agent was with him).

But they came back with an empty truck. First, all the shops in Zhudong district were closed. Then, they went to talk to Mayor Ho, who called the Mayor of the Guanxi Town to lend some rice to us. They went to Guanxi and borrowed a half a truckload of rice.

But they were stopped by a group of disorderly people in the street who took the rice from the truck and burned it on the street. They let the truck go only because Gong Wenyu was Taiwanese.

The next day, Zhao Xianrui called, and according to the information of his informers, mobs in Taipei demonstrated in front of the headquarter building, robbed the police station's guns, burned the Public Sales Bureau, and beat provincial officials who came from mainland China after Taiwan was returned to China when Japan retreated.

On the third day, Zhao Xianrui did not call, and my father called him and Mayor Ho's office, but no one answered. The phone was no longer available. The only externally connected phone had been cut off. We were isolated from the outside world and did not learn about the aftermath of the February 28 Incident until later.

My father told Zhang Xueliang about these conditions.

After receiving the phone call from Zhao Xianrui on the first day, my father called the military intelligence bureau station's chief of the Taipei Station (台北站), Lin Dingli. After that, Liu Guoqing (劉果青), the savvy and capable deputy head of the station, reported the latest information to my father.

Fortunately, the Taipei station had only been in Taiwan for two years. They came to Taiwan the first day after Taiwan was returned to China from Japan in 1945.

The first thing they did was establish a very wide network of informers, who knew all that was going on.

Liu Guoqing told my father:

1. Most Taiwanese were hardworking; only a few small groups were making trouble. After Japan's

surrender, about 200,000 Taiwanese Japanese soldiers were left in Taiwan. They had retreated from Hainan Island. The government sent all of them to their original hometowns to farm their own land. But a few troublemakers didn't want to go home to farm; they stayed in the town. What could they do? Either be a rogue or an informer. They organized in small groups, maybe a sergeant commanded less than twenty people. The same people would steal guns and inform Liu Guoqing where they would do it.

2. The Communist Party had no activity in Taiwan. There was only one female, Xie Xuehong (謝雪紅), who was a Communist with some reputation in Taiwan. They only had one small underground party that had been established recently, including Yang Kehuang (楊克煌), Su Xin (蘇新), Cha Zimin (察子民), Wu Ketai (吳克泰), and a total of about twenty people.

My father also sent a military policeman who could speak the Hakka and Minnan languages. He lent him my British-made Phillips bicycle and told him to wear plain clothes to go out and inquire about the news. After a long time, he came back with his clothes torn into one-inch strips. He said that he was beaten by the mob and had to come back. But there were no injuries on his body. Is it that those who attacked him were very measured? When they hit him, they only tore his clothes, inch by inch, and didn't grab my bicycle (thank you!). Or maybe he rode into a Taoshan tunnel and found a corner where he spent three hours tearing his clothes into thin strips?

HOW TO ADAPT

This is what Father knew:

1. Some Taiwanese in the cities had beaten up the people who recently came to Taiwan from mainland China (considered "outsiders," 外省人), and they had taken some guns from the police station.
2. The "mountain people" living around us were peaceful.
3. The two army divisions sent by Chiang Kai-shek to Taiwan had been called back, because of poor discipline. Taiwan only had one regiment of military police to keep the peace for the whole island (the fourth regiment, one platoon, was assigned to my father).
4. In addition, there were separate troops in the Keelung Fortress and the Kaohsiung Fortress, commanded by the Commander of the Fortress, but they were only responsible for guarding the fortress.

We didn't know how long the turmoil would last. My father invited Zhao Wanghua (趙旺華) to drink. He was the director of the Qingquan Police Station and was also the chief of the local tribe. He only spoke the dialect of the mountain and Japanese. My father hired a translator, Xiao, to help.

They drank over a large plate of fried rice noodles.

The main thing was to keep the "mountain people" on

our side, buy sweet potatoes from them, and inquire about the news. They happily sold the sweet potatoes to us, but they didn't have any outside news.

At that time, there were only two or three generals in Taiwan. Zhao Wanghua liked his drink. After drinking two bottles of sake, he would hold up his left hand and shout, "Long live Major General Liu!" His right hand would hold another wine bottle! My father felt secure.

My father's strategy was (1) invite Zhao Wenhua to drink every day, (2) place a bronze warning bell between the military police barracks on the other side and the police station, (3) order the military police to send a machine gun with three soldiers to block the Taoshan Tunnel five kilometers away to keep us safe, and (4) send half of the rice from the large kitchen (the one for the agents) to the small kitchen (the one for Mr. Zhang and us). Everyone had a sweet potato meal. The large kitchen had a lot of sweet potato with a little rice, and the small kitchen had a lot of rice with few sweet potatoes.

We had a good time when we ate. Mr. Zhang and we all ate sweet potato rice.

Miss Four ate white rice only. To serve the rice, the waiter's spoons had holes, so the rice would separate from the potatoes. I think it was my mother who taught the waiter this trick. Zhang Xueliang would eat a lot of rice with a few potatoes. The team workers, who ate in their own dining room, ate mostly potatoes with only a little rice. In our family, we ate more potatoes than rice. The waiter would serve each of us this way.

There was no problem with the dishes. We ate a lot of Hsinchu rice noodles, Taishan winter bamboo shoots, black caviar, Jinhua preserved hams, mushroom, shrimp, scallops, and sea cucumber. We didn't have vegetables and fruits. Some of my mother's chickens also were on the menu. Scrambled eggs were always eaten very quickly, so Mother told the chef to add more salt when he scrambled the eggs to make them last longer. Her chickens just couldn't keep up with laying eggs. (As you can see, my mother was always thinking.)

Figure 22 Zhao Yidi feeding Mother's chickens

A SPY IS CAUGHT - MARCH 4, 1947

On March 4, 1947, the military police at the Taishan tunnel caught a man and sent him to the agents for questioning. The man walked from the outside to the entrance of the tunnel and looked around. The military police asked him where he was going. He said that he wanted to go into the mountains. The police asked if he had a permit. At that time, outside people had to get a pass at the Zhudong Police Station to get into the mountain. He said no. Deputy Xiong questioned him and got nowhere. My father saw that the person looked like a veteran who had been a Japanese soldier but decided to let him go.

My father asked the small kitchen to send a large bowl of white rice, topped with winter bamboo shoots and fried pork for him to eat, and arranged for him to walk through our compound to see a lot of agents with box guns. Then, two agents holding box guns took him in a Jeep to the tunnel and let him go.

My father suspected this guy was a spy sent here to observe our manpower and firepower. So, he decided to let him see it, and scare him away! Sun Tzu's *The Art of War* says, "The supreme art of war is to subdue the enemy without fighting."

On the afternoon of March 4, Zhao Xianrui stationed at Zhudong came back. He drove a large truck with a lot of rice and flour.

After the phone was cut off on March 1, he had not been idle. He contacted his informers and learned that Communist Party member Wu Ketai and some of his fellows had come to Zhudong, preparing to enter the mountain and rescue Zhang Xueliang.

He immediately went to the Mayor of Zhudong district to discuss this with him. My father had a good relationship with Mayor Ho. He was very helpful. He gave a big truck loaded with rice and flour to Zhao to return to Qingquan. The basic training of the agents was martial arts, shooting, and driving. But Zhao Xianrui had not driven for more than ten years. Luckily, he had the whole mountain highway for himself and finally got to the Qingquan without falling down into a deep ravine!

However, he had an eventful trip. When driving away, a group of lawless people set fire to the Mayor's office. Zhao stepped on the gas pedal and tried to flee. But a mob with long rifles came after him. He pulled out his box shell gun and shot with his left hand from the window while driving. His aim was not good. Fortunately, the box gun could fire twenty bullets at one time. He first sent four or five bullets to the leader of the group. The man fell. The others ran away very fast. He stepped on the gas pedal and drove away, leaving behind a guy bleeding on the ground. He didn't know if he died or not.

When Zhao arrived, he became the hero of the agents, not because he shot with his left hand, but because he brought back white rice!

After he reported what happened, my father told the deputy to immediately strengthen the alert. Usually, Zhang Xueliang had no guards during the day. Following this incident, he had two guards standing five feet away from the front and right corridors, with the box gun, and two guards were assigned to the gate. Zhang Fucheng was also sent with his light machine gun and two agents to the Taoshan Tunnel to reinforce the military police already there. They needed more eyes and ears, so that they could take turns to sleep.

Then my father went to tell Zhang Xueliang that Zhudong had been in trouble with the people and burned the district office. Zhao Xianrui brought a truck and some rice and flour.

He didn't tell Zhang Xueliang that there were Communist Party members who wanted to enter the mountain to rescue him.

MIDNIGHT HORROR - MARCH 4-5, 1947

On the evening of the same day (March 4), the alarm on the other side of the river suddenly rang—this was a signal of a dangerous situation! Everyone got up and put on clothes and shoes. Six agents took positions outside of Zhang Xueliang's room with box guns, two were outside of our room, and other agents all took positions designated for an emergency. My father wore his military uniform and put a revolver and a box gun on his waist. We slept in the first two rooms of the left wing, the third room was my father's office, where he had a carbine gun in the closet. He went over to get it. When he walked over, he saw a man crawling on the ground. My father immediately pulled out his revolver and shot at the head of the man on the ground. He heard a scream, and the head stopped moving! My father knew the man was not one of our agents, because no one was allowed into the rooms where Zhang Xueliang or my father lived.

The "man" turned out to be a chicken raised by Mother. One of them had come in and slept in the empty waste basket. In a hurry, it turned over the basket and ran with it. In the dark, it looked like a person crawling. My father took a shot in the dark and hit the "man's" head. But, no! It was a shot in the dark that hit the head of the chicken, or maybe the chicken itself.

My father quickly told the agents outside that it was a misfire. He told us to sit in a room. Then he went to Zhang Xueliang and told him the gun shot was a misfire. He found four of them had already dressed and put on their shoes. Mr. Zhang, Miss Four, and Wu Ma were sitting in the living room. The bodyguard Du Fa stood outside the

155

paper door of the room and blocked my father's way. Don't forget that Du's hand was as big as a bowl! My father never carried a gun when he went to see Zhang Xueliang, and he entered the room to talk to him.

When Dad came back, he immediately summoned the Deputy and three or four senior agents to meet in the study. I took a look and didn't dare to go in.

According to the information that they knew, the analysis was: (1) If someone came to attack, they were likely part of the Communist Party led by Wu Ketai. Their numbers were few and they didn't have much fire power. They couldn't enter the Taoshan Tunnel, and if they did get in, we could overpower them. (2) It most likely was not the mountain people. If it were them, we were in big trouble! We would have two choices: stay, or run.

My father's conclusion was to stay and protect Zhang Xueliang. Mr. Zhang's room was the center. From there to the bridge, he placed three lines of defense: more agents outside the room, a few agents at the bridge, and the military police would guard the other side of the wooden bridge and the suspension bridge. The purpose was to prevent Zhang Xueliang from being rescued.

If the mountain people were against us, we could only run. We weren't afraid that they would come in the middle of the night to cut off our heads with their long knives; we were afraid that they would not sell sweet potatoes to us.

My father sent two agents to accompany the drivers Gong Wenyu and Zhang Yilong to cross the river to fill our small jeep and big truck with gasoline and to wait. In case we had to run, they could drive to Keelung Fortress to get reinforcements.

After the meeting, my father went to Zhang Xueliang

to inform him about the situation and asked Mr. Zhang and Miss Four to prepare a small suitcase in case we had to leave immediately.

My father went back to the room to see us; he made sure that we were all dressed. He didn't have to ask us to put our shoes on and didn't ask Mother to prepare a suitcase; he didn't say anything. I didn't know if we would go with them or not, as the space on the truck would probably be filled with agents and all their firepower.

In the room, there was a small altar six inches above the floor which was used for meditation and hanging important pictures. My mother sat on the edge and held my youngest brother, Alex (who was three years old) in her lap.

Zhang Xueliang walked in holding a flashlight covered with his hand. Miss Four hung on his arm tightly, and they had a small red suitcase with them.

Mr. Zhang put down the suitcase, sat down close to my mother, and told her, "If you hear a gun shot, you have to lie down. But you are sitting very low now; it is okay, very good!"

My father was also in the room. They didn't talk to each other. It seems that Mr. Zhang asked my father, "We are prepared. Is this suitcase small enough?" and then they went back to their side of the room with the little red suitcase.

It turned out to be a false alarm! Two mountain people had used poison to fish in the river in the middle of the night. The police on duty saw a torch at the river and asked for the password. When he didn't get an answer, he fired a shot at the torch. The two men tossed the torch in the water and ran away. So, the military police hit the bell repeatedly as was instructed to report an emergency.

From Zhang Xueliang's diary:

March 1 (1947)

Liu Yiguan told me that in the riots, the Taiwan people attacked the government building and beat the 外省人 (non-Taiwanese outsiders).

March 5th

Suddenly, Zhao Xianrui came with a truck last night, brought rice flours, etc....all of a sudden it seemed the enemy was coming, outside my window covered with guards, and all armed with weapons. What was happening? I asked Old Liu to come over to ask him, but he didn't come. I saw that they burned documents, packed their bags, and the people were chaotic. What happened? Why doesn't he tell me about it? I went to his room to see him and found out he was very panicky.

March 7

Today, they are sneaking around. In the early morning, Mrs. Liu came and pretended to look around, and there must be something outside. I think it's nothing more than that. I fell into a deep sleep.

March 8

In the early morning, Mrs. Liu snuck around again. She pretended to borrow cigarettes. It was ridiculous. When we were eating, Old Liu didn't come; he tried to avoid seeing me. I was very angry. I treated them with sincerity and guided them with good words. They should tell me everything happening. But they were just sneaking and play tricks on me. Later, I thought about it, that was his job. Later, I thought again, "A gentleman could be killed but not insulted." His rude and dishonest move is really irritating.

March 17
In the last few days, Chief Liu told me about the crisis
about Taiwan. It's really sad to hear about the corruption
of the officers that I've talked about in the past few days.
Corruption among officials is not a small crime. The Tai-
wanese have a lot of admiration for this move, but there are
many that could be criticized.

HUGE DIFFERENCE IN INTERPRETATIONS

In fact, the same events, because of different positions
and different moods, could be interpreted very differently.
On March 7 and 8, the two days after the above-mentioned midnight horror, my father couldn't talk to Zhang
Xueliang because he had no new information. He certainly
couldn't tell him that some Communist Party members
tried to rescue him. He could only ignore him, so he asked
Mother to visit Mr. Zhang and Miss Four and say hello.
If everyone could be normal, they could just nod to each
other. However, the good intentions of my parents became
"sneaking and stupid." My mother was very smart; she
could feel Miss Four's coldness.

Zhang Xueliang may have suspected that my father
had orders to kill him to prevent him from being rescued by
external forces if the situation was urgent. With his experience
and situation, I could guess that Zhang Xueliang already
knew Chiang Kai-shek had orders for what to do with him.

Zhang Xueliang said in his oral history, that during his
surgery in Guiyang, someone wanted to buy a doctor to kill
him. And instructions had been given that Zhang Xueliang
couldn't be rescued alive.

Chapter Twenty-Four

It was a close call during the "midnight crisis." My father had a staff meeting with five of his most important staff, leaving instructions to kill Zhang Xueliang instead of allowing him to be rescued by his supporters. It appeared that one of his staff, who often received big stacks of money from Zhang Xueliang, might have told him about these orders.

What happened was after the meeting, my father went to Zhang Xueliang and told him there were two choices, to stay or go, depending on how the situation developed. If we were to go, because there was only one small Jeep and a truck, my father would lead about twenty of his best agents to protect Zhang Xueliang and Miss Four. They would be asked to take only one small suitcase. Deputy Xiong would stay behind to take care of all the remaining people, including my mother and us children.

After the "midnight crisis," there were no further incidents until March 10. On March 11, we got telephone service back. We learned that the Nationalist army had landed at the Port of Keelung on March 9 and had the situation under control. During the twelve days in the mountain, we lived in the dark, but it turned out my father had made all the right decisions in the dark (with no information).

After the February 28 Incident, Zhang Xueliang's mentality changed. It was not easy for my father and mother to get along with him. Everyone lived under one roof and ate at the same table. We children were still the same. My father always talked little, but now Mr. Zhang talked little too, and the atmosphere at the table was not right. So, my mother and Miss Four tried hard to carry on conversations at the table.

My mother always helped my father; she was a very self-respecting person. She was very good to Mr. Zhang and Miss Four, but she did not make small talk, so the psychological pressure was very heavy. She often wondered if she had done enough. Did the children wake Mr. Zhang and Miss Four when we cried? Since the rooms were separated by five rooms and eight walls, Mr. Zhang probably did not hear us. But Mother did not know, and she wondered; the pressure was very high. She couldn't sleep well, and she often quarreled with my father. After seven or eight months under the pressure, she mentally broke down. In October 1947, she went to the Taipei University of Taiwan Affiliated Hospital for examination. The doctor said my mother may be depressed and needed to be hospitalized for treatment.

In August 1947, in order for me to go to Taipei for junior high school, my father had asked Commander Peng Mengji (彭孟緝司令) to give us a house in Taipei.

My father sent machine gunner Zhang Fucheng (張富成) and a middle-aged maid to accompany me.

This time, my father took a month off, and stayed in "my" house. He arranged for my mother to check into the best hospital in Taipei.

They used drugs to calm her mood. She went home three weeks later, spent a week of recuperation in Taipei, and returned to Qingquan. She was completely cured.

However, my mother was labelled mentally ill (神經病) and "a crazy woman" (瘋婆子), and was always called "Liu Yiguang's old woman" (not even given a name). People spread this rumor and drama about my mother, which was untrue.

This is another reason why I wrote this book in my 80s, to rehabilitate my mother's reputation.

Figure 23 Mother at desk

Chapter Twenty-Five

EVALUATION OF THE FEBRUARY 28 INCIDENT (二二八事變) IN TAIWAN

On October 17, 1945, the Seventh Army of the Nationalist Army boarded the U.S. Navy ship in Keelung. It was a glorious and solemn task on behalf of China to recover Taiwan after Japan surrendered it, after occupying it for fifty years. The Nationalist army was going to land, the pier was crowded with men, women, and children who all welcomed the leader, most of them spontaneous and full of enthusiasm and expectation.

Here they came! Here they came! A group of "grandmother" soldiers (婆婆兵) came down from the stairs. They wore heavy cotton jackets, held tightly to the rails of the stairs, moving one foot after another. They were the officers and soldiers of our honorable army to receive Taiwan! They were fifteen and sixteen to thirty-four years old. The older ones were cooks who could live to over thirty years, while the younger ones were soldiers, replacing other soldiers who had been killed.

The Nationalist Government sent Chen Yi (陳儀) to Taiwan as the ruler. Gone was Japan's dictator; in came a Chinese one. Among the nine important deputy directors of the nine important offices of the Chief Executive, only one deputy director was a Taiwanese, because for the Chinese, Taiwanese were considered inferior.

At the end of the war, Taiwan's industrial and agricultural production was in a state of paralysis, due to a lack of materials, a serious shortage of rice, soaring prices, a slack industry, a large number of people unemployed, and a deterioration in public security. After Chen Yi arrived, all the enterprises owned by the Japanese were accepted in the name of "state-owned capital," and these enterprises monopolized Taiwan's industries, in finance, trade, and other fields. The Taiwanese Chief Executive also set up a trade bureau and a monopoly bureau to compete with the people.

The officers from mainland China were corrupt, and the army was rude and behaved badly toward the Taiwanese. After one year, the two armies were transferred back to the mainland, leaving only the fourth regiment of the military police to maintain security in Taiwan (one platoon had been assigned to my father).

A forty-year-old widow set up an illegal candy stall on the street to sell cigarettes (only the government could sell cigarettes) to raise her son and daughter. One day, on February 27, 1947, she was accidentally shot by an inspector, which precipitated the February 28 Incident.

TROUBLEMAKERS

After Japan's surrender, about 200,000 Taiwanese Japanese soldiers remained in Taiwan, who retreated from Hainan Island. As mentioned before, a few troublemakers who didn't want to go home to far, hung around and robbed people. They gathered in groups, went to the police station and the armory to rob guns, burned the monopoly bureau, and surrounded the office. They beat up people who recently came to Taiwan from mainland China and killed more than 1,000 people in two weeks. But most Taiwanese opened their doors to protect them.

These troublemakers were cruel people. Our classmate Hu Xianwu (胡憲武) told us his personal experience:

> On February 28, 1947, his mother took the children to the shore in Keelung. His father came to Taiwan as a high-ranking official. After he settled down, he arranged to get his family to Taiwan. The Taiwanese driver came to pick them up. The dock was already in chaos. The driver was alert. When he had driven a short distance, he turned back to City Hall and told them to get off at City Hall to take refuge. Then he saw that a young mother sitting in a rickshaw with her baby was stopped. Some people used Taiwanese and Japanese to ask questions, which she could not understand. Two people wearing Japanese clothes (they were the organized rogues who had been retreated from Hainan Island) grabbed the baby from the mother's hands. Each took one hand and one foot and tore him into two parts! And killed the crying mother!

> His mother quickly took them to City Hall and
> said in Shanghainese, "We are Shanghai people!"
> The guards saw that their children wore robes and
> told them to go over to where a bunch of refugees
> sat together inside and told them to keep quiet.

The troublemakers started a local event, but the governor Chen Yi exaggerated it as a major event in an effort to overthrow the Nationalist government. So, Chiang Kai-shek sent twenty-one corps (軍, each was 10,000 soldiers) to Taiwan to suppress the masses. After disembarking in Keelung, they used their machine guns to shoot people on the docks and the streets, and then advanced to Taipei. They continued south, and the police followed to arrest people and put them in jail. The crackdown on the Taiwanese rebellion was extremely harsh.

On March 17, 1947, the Minister of National Defense Bai Chongxi (白崇禧) came to Taiwan under the command of Chiang Kai-shek. He found out the February 28 Incident was a local event, not a movement to overthrow the government.

Afterwards, the estimated casualties were various:

Yang Lianggong's (楊亮功) investigation reported 190 people killed and 1,761 people injured. Bai Chongxi (白崇禧) reported 1,860 people were killed or injured. The New York Times Hobman Nanjing report stated 2,200 people died. The Taiwan Police General Command reported 3,200 people died.

The big lie was that up to 100,000 Taiwanese were killed and that about 1,000 mainland Chinese were killed. It is generally estimated to be from more than 800 to 20,000 people. The people from other provinces who died totalled about 1,000.

It was a local event, but the Democratic Progressive Party made it a cash box. For sixty years, they paid the victims reparations, and Ma Yingjiu (馬英九), former president of the Republic of China, was the leader.

Chapter Twenty-Six

Zhang Xueliang said later, "For several days, Chief Liu told me what really happened in the February 28 Incident. The corruption of the top officers created the sad consequence. The Taiwanese did some of they should do, but many things could be criticized."

MO DEHUI'S VISIT

On May 12, 1947, Mo Dehui (莫德惠), a member of the Northeast Central Committee, came to Qingquan to see Zhang Xueliang with the permission of Chiang Kai-shek. He gave Zhang Xueliang a radio and a battery-operated juice maker. Mo lived in Qingquan for six days. Every day, he talked with Zhang Xueliang for hours, and a lot of pictures were taken. These were the first pictures shown to the outside world after Zhang Xueliang's house arrest.

In the picture, Mr. Zhang is the one with his hands in his pocket, standing next to two women. The thin one was Miss Four, and the other was my mother. The big man on the left is Mo Dehui. On the right at the lower step is my father. I stood above him. I was thirteen years old.

Figure 24 Liu Family with Zhang Xueliang and Mo Dehui

The three children were my sister (six years old), big man Frank (four years old) and small man Alex (two years old). On my left was Wu Ma. The other three were wearing "plain clothes." There were eighteen steps between the two terraces. The house behind me was the residence of Mr. Zhang. It was three meters higher than the platform of the tennis court and the staff quarters. The place where I stood is where a guard stood watch at night. During the February 28 Incident, there were eight guards at this platform, six were on the side of Mr. Zhang, and two at my father's side.

The hill at the back was a very steep forest. Only monkeys could go up and down.

Figure 25 l to r: my father, Miss Four, Zhang Xueliang, and Mo Dehui

The tennis photo of Mo Dehui's visit was widely posted to the outside world, but Mo Dehui never played tennis. Zhang Xueliang played tennis very well, and Miss Four didn't play. My father always played against Mr. Zhang in the clothes he was wearing, a suit trouser and rolled-up shirt. He did wear tennis shoes.

Chapter Twenty-Seven

GENERAL ZHANG ZHIZHONG'S REPORT

In October 1947, when my mother was hospitalized, my father asked for one month absence from his work to take care of my mother. The director of the Bureau, Mao Renfeng, sent the two-star general Zhang Yanfo (張嚴佛), the Number Two man of the Bureau, to replace my father for one month. He arrived in Qingquan (清泉) on October 2, 1947. Zhang Yanfo arranged for three-star general Zhang Zhizhong (張志忠) to visit two days before he reported to work. Zhang Zhizhong and Zhang Yanfo talked for two or three hours. After a month, Zhang Yanfo wrote a report to Chiang Kai-shek.

In his report entitled, "The Process of Imprisonment of Zhang Xueliang by the Bureau of Secrecy," Zhang Yanfo said that Zhang Xueliang told him that Liu Yiguang and his family treated him and Miss Four very badly. He reported that Zhang Xueliang asked him to report to Chiang Kai-shek, with two requests:

175

1. Hope to restore freedom,
2. Ask that Liu Yiguang and his family be moved out of his residence.

It was basically a prisoner asking to be freed. If that couldn't happen, then please change the jail keeper.

Figure 26 front l to r: Mao Renfeng, Zhang Xueliang; back l to r: Liu Yiguang and unidentified man

Was Zhang Xueliang stupid? If he could gain his freedom, what did he care where Liu Yiguang and his family went?

In fact, these two points were made up by Zhang Yanfo and Zhang Zhizhong. The real reason was to get our family out of the way.

Zhang Zhizhong went to see Chiang Kai-shek. Chiang Kai-shek was unhappy and undecided. Zhang Zhizhong went to see Madame Chiang. She first said (using their nicknames), "Wenbo (文伯), we are sorry for Zhang Hanqing (漢卿)."

Madame Chiang saw Zhang Xueliang's request for freedom. She said, "This is not easy to do. I am afraid I can't get permission now." As for asking for the removal of Liu Yiguang's family, she said, "I could find a way to do it."

At the end of November 1947, when Zhang Zhizhong returned from Qingquan for less than a month, my father received an order from the Bureau and was transferred to take over as the general captain of the Hangzhou Traffic Police Corps (more than 10,000 people).

At our home in Taipei, our luggage was packed and placed in the living room; we were ready to go.

At the beginning of December, my father received an order from Chiang Kai-shek to see him. My father went to Nanjing. Chiang Kai-shek told my father, "You go back. Without my approval, no one can make the decision who is to watch Zhang Xueliang." My father came back, continued to be his major general, Commissioner Liu, and continued to accompany Zhang Xueliang.

General Zhang Zhizhong's attempt to replace my father to accompany Zhang Xueliang failed. But his report become what the general public believed, and the bad name was tied to my family forever!

Chapter Twenty-Eight

SNAKE STORIES

Qingquan is a neighborhood of Taiwan known for its hot springs. Located in a tropical rainforest, it is very humid and hot, and there are a lot of snakes. Zhang Xueliang and my father's group lived there for eleven years, and they had many snake stories.

When they first arrived, snakes were all over—on the ground and up in the trees. One agent was walking and saw a big snake in front of him. He bent over the roadside to pick up a pole to fight the snake. The pole moved; it turned out to be a snake. One agent went to open the gate in the morning. When he reached out, he grabbed a snake. The guards on duty to guard the gate had to bring a bamboo pole in addition to their guns. To hit a snake, you had to use a flexible stick, not a wooden one.

The venomous green snake (青竹絲) was the most dangerous. It stayed on the green tree where it was hard to

179

see. The most venomous snake was the pit viper (trimere-surus mucrosquamatus, 龜殼花).

There were also nonvenomous snakes, like water snakes and pythons. The big pythons could swallow a young deer without long horns. It would digest it for one month just lying there. I once saw a snake about one-and-half-meters long. It didn't move on the ground. When I saw that it had a snake tail in its mouth, I realized it had actually swallowed another snake the same length; it was so full that it couldn't move!

People are afraid of snakes. In fact, snakes are more afraid of people. Snakes attack people or big animals for self-defense. What is the use of biting you? People are too big to eat!

Later, we had more people, and the snakes were fewer, but in the ditch under the rock wall in the back of the dormitory, a lot of snakes were crowded together. When I looked at them, my skin grew goosebumps.

Would the snakes climb into the house? The sub team leader Huang Xuan (黃玄) was a fat man. He slept in the summer without a cover. One night in his sleep, he felt his belly was cold. A snake was on his belly, enjoying the warmth. He shouted and jumped out of bed, but fortunately the snake did not bite him.

One day, Zhang Xueliang's bodyguard Du Fa went to the hot springs to take a bath. Suddenly, a big snake climbed in the room, and he jumped up and ran out naked, calling loudly "Help! Help!" He forgot all about his kung fu! He was a Northeasterner and had never seen a "long worm!" (長蟲).

One day, while we ate, Zhou Yongxun (周雍遜) sat with his back to a window. Mr. Zhang calmly said to him, "Don't move. When I call you, immediately stand up and run!" After Zhou did just that, we saw a red snake come out of the window lock hole, ready to bite! The waiter killed the snake. The locals said that this extremely venomous red snake always came in pairs. If one disappeared, the other one would come to look for it. Sure enough, the next day another one came out from the same window hole. Our waiter was waiting and killed it too.

When my number five brother "Big Barbarian" Frank (劉季森) was less than six years old, he went to the other side of the river to watch the military police play basketball. He sat on a piece of wood. When he stepped down, he stepped on the head of a snake. He wore shorts. The snake wrapped around his bare leg. My brother kept his foot on the snake's head and did not panic. He took out a half of a pair of scissors (he had different magic weapons in his pocket every day, but fortunately, this time it was not a living frog). His left hand grabbed the snake tail, while his right hand cut the snake inch-by-inch toward his leg, leaving only a piece of skin. If he cut it all the way through, he would cut his own leg. When the snake stopped moving, he loosened his feet. As he looked up, he saw a group of military police staring at him. They were so stunned and afraid to disturb him. He had fought the snake so calmly; he sure was the son of my father!

The holes in the stone wall at our place were the best hiding spots for snakes. But Frank often looked for snakes in the stone wall and grabbed the snake's tail to pull it out. The snakes had scales and couldn't be pulled out. It didn't matter. Later, there were fewer snakes on the stone wall. The snakes must have talked to each other: "'Big Barbarian' is coming, we better just go.

The creek in Qingquan was small and we couldn't swim in it. There was a natural rock dike in the upper reaches of the bridge. The water level grew higher and formed a small pool. The women of the local people washed their clothes there. One day, I was with Li Yunzhang (李蘊章), daughter of my father's friend, the former Kaiyang County mayor Li Yuzhen. We called her Little Sister Li (李小妹). She was eleven years old, living at our home and going to school in Taipei.

Mr. Zhang and a group of people walked to the bank. They disturbed the ground. A big water snake rushed out of a hole. My number six brother was with the group; he pointed and called out "snake!" I saw the large snake directly swinging toward me. Little Sister Li, who held my hands, turned around and saw the snake, and her "qigong" came in handy as she climbed up the tree (my body) and stood on top of my shoulder! The snake was feet away from me before it turned and fled from us.

The snake was not swimming, it was sliding over the water. The large snake had filled itself with "qi," or energy, and became larger. It used its natural survival ability when faced with life-threatening danger.

When I came ashore, I saw Mr. Zhang take off his shorts and throw them to Du Fa. Mr. Zhang did not wear underwear. He went down to the direction of the girls who were there washing clothes. Afraid to wet his shirt, he lifted it with both hands, making his body easier to see. The girls all lowered their heads, laughing. A new agent asked me if Mr. Zhang was crazy. I shook my head. Mr. Zhang was very normal! The gentleman was open and poised; he hid nothing. He told us more than once that he rarely wore underwear and never wore clothes when he slept. He said that not wearing clothes to sleep was healthy.

Because of Mr. Zhang's casual attitude in front of the girls, the locals spread a story that was repeated many times and exaggerated out of proportion. There was a local man in his forties who seemed honest. He said that when he was a kid, he often saw Zhang Xueliang swimming in the river naked. Mr. Zhang was not an indecent man.

Chapter Twenty-Nine

BACK TO NORMAL:
DAILY LIFE IN QINGQUAN

In November 1947, Father brought my mother back from the hospital to Qingquan. Mr. Zhang's attitude toward my mother was greatly improved. He probably felt some sympathy and slight guilt for my mother's illness.

It was almost a year since the February 28 Incident. Later, Zhang Xueliang would know that my father was doing the right things and did his best to protect him, in a situation with no information.

Mr. Zhang was a great-hearted person. When his bad feeling was gone, the sun shone! He started to speak loudly again, my mother didn't feel nervous anymore, and everything went back to normal.

I was happiest in the Lunar New Year that year. I won 40,000 Taiwan dollars playing cards with Mr. Zhang. I wrote to my older brothers in Chongqing, saying, "I can buy whatever I wish." And I did buy a Parker pen for 10,000 Taiwan dollars. When I filled the ink for the first time, I pointed the tip of the pen to the bottom of the bottle and pushed down very hard and bent the tip of the pen! I didn't write one word with my new pen, not even the word, "stupid"!

Figure 27 Zhang Xueliang and Miss Four playing cards; Theresa looking on

At the end of 1947, after my father took Mother and us kids back to Qingquan, Mr. Zhang had returned to his normal self. At the dinner, he spoke aloud again, and my mother was not nervous anymore.

❊ ❊ ❊

Mr. Zhang and Miss Four ate their breakfast in their room: fried eggs and bread and butter. The waiter cooked and brought it to them. Mr. Zhang always sat at the desk in the corridor in the morning to read and write. There were clear windows and flowers, and he looked up at the green mountains.

They came out before lunch. When Miss Four saw my mother, she would say, "Mrs. Liu, did you ("你") sleep well?" My mother would reply, "Okay, Miss Four did you ("您") (using the formal polite form of saying "you") sleep well?"

Mr. Zhang always took a nap after lunch. Before three o'clock, his bodyguard Du Fa would walk around the dining room area. He wore cotton shoes and walked without sound. The purpose was to prevent others from entering Mr. Zhang's side.

Mr. Zhang would play tennis every afternoon. There would be a heavy rain every day in the mountains for three minutes. Thirteen-year-old ("Captain of the Ducks") Wang Shizhong and I would take a broom to wipe the water off the court. Nobody assigned me that job.

Figure 28 Liu family walk; Zhao Yidi joins

187

They played doubles, Mr. Zhang and my father on each side, and two agents would accompany them, the better one on my father's side.

Wang Shizhong picked up the ball. Why was he always picking up the ball on my father's side? Because Mr. Zhang could always return the shot.

Figure 29 Zhang Xueliang with pockets for candy

Mr. Zhang would take a walk after dinner every day. He always walked in front, followed by Miss Four, my father and us kids, and then the bodyguard Old Du, then five or six agents, and at the end was the platoon leader of the military police.

They only carried a small pistol behind the waist under the plain clothes so that Mr. Zhang would not see it. Mr. Zhang always talked out loud, walked out of the gate, crossed the bridge, and bought some candy at a small shop in the end of the bridge. Miss Four sewed clothes for him. He had large pockets for the candy he brought every day. He didn't give them to us kids; he mostly just threw it away. Because he disturbed the business of the little shop, he would have to buy things.

After going out, Mr. Zhang would walk about one kilometer along the road and turn back before the road got steep.

❈ ❈ ❈

The mountain was quiet. Zhang Xueliang wrote in a diary every day. My father also wrote in a diary every day. It was part of his job, and Dai Li's instructions were to watch Zhang Xueliang's every word and action, and to report in writing every two weeks. My mother often wrote in a diary. I didn't peek in my father's diary, though I did read my mother's diary. Once she wrote, "At the right time, open your giant eyes. Monkey Mountain shrouded by layers of clouds "及時疏巨目，猴山堆層雲.

I changed it to, "Open your eyes at the right moment. Monkey Mountain often has clouds" (及時應疏目，猴山常堆雲). I later wrote in a diary, complaining that I always got my number two brother's old clothes. He wrote in his diary, "Number Three is unwilling to sit in the second row now."

❈ ❈ ❈

By the summer of 1948, I went to school at Taipei Jianguo Middle School and my sister and younger brothers also went to school in Taipei. We got a house near the center of the business zone, in a Japanese-style house with a yard.

My mother raised chickens in the backyard. Every winter, she still smoked Hunan bacon with cypress branches next to the henhouse. Two of the trees were gifts for Mr. Zhang.

This house was also the guest house for the agents who came to Taipei. They would stay in the tatami rooms, several to a room under a mosquito net. Once we had twenty-seven people in the house and Little Wang and I had to sleep horizontally on the feet of six agents.

My mother would cook a fatty pork dish for them.

Figure 30 Mother cooking in Taipei kitchen

My mother's chickens began to lay eggs, and we ate steamed egg soup now and then.

When one of us had a birthday, we would all have a bowl of noodles, and the birthday kid would have a poached egg in the bowl. When the chickens were too old to lay eggs, we could have stewed chicken! We had unwritten rules when eating chicken: Theresa (my father called my sister "girl," 女孩子) ate one chicken leg, Alex ate the other leg, Frank and I each got a wing, and my mother ate the chicken head and half of the neck.

My mother always wanted us kids to eat better and devoted herself to my father. She never had a good day for herself. She never complained, but she hardly smiled either. My father had his career, and we each later had a professional career and wonderful families. What about my mother? During the War of Resistance against Japan, she ate rice with tea in the mainland, saying that Hunanese liked rice with tea. After arriving in Taiwan, it was not much better. She ate chicken bones, saying they contained calcium.

Her only entertainment was playing mahjong, to accompany Mr. Zhang and Miss Four (Wu Ma would be the fourth player).

Chapter Thirty

MOVE TO KAOHSIUNG:
February – December 1949

On February 1, 1949, President Chiang Kai-shek stepped down. Prior to that, he had appointed Chen Cheng (陳誠) as Governor of Taiwan Province.

When the President in charge Li Zongren (李宗仁) decided to release Zhang Xueliang and Yang Hucheng, he announced it in the national newspapers. Both Zhang Xueliang and my father saw the news.

But my father got the order to discuss it with Governor Chen Cheng. He told my father to move Zhang Xueliang secretly to Kaohsiung. My father flew Zhang Xueliang and Miss Four the same day to Kaohsiung Fortress. He only took a small group of agents with them.

When President in Charge's special envoy Cheng Siyuan (程思遠) went to the Taiwan to see Governor Chen, he said he didn't know where Zhang Xueliang was.[13]

---

13 . Chen Lübei 陳履碚, the third son of Chen Cheng told me: after his father died, they found a handwritten letter from Chiang Kai-shek instructing him to deal with the release of Zhang

My father's group occupied the headquarters on top of Shou Mountain (壽山) and the fortress commander Peng Mengqi (彭孟緝) moved to a lower place.

The fortress headquarters was not suitable for living. There were three offices downstairs; Father live in two, and Du Fa lived in one. The three offices upstairs were for Mr. Zhang, Miss Four, and Wu Ma. Mr. Zhang, Miss Four, and my father ate their lunch and dinner at a rectangular table against the wall outside of the building.

I also lived there on summer vacation. My deepest impression was that every morning, there were many white spots on the blue sea, which were bamboo sails going out to sea to fish. Every afternoon, I went down the mountain to swim in Xizi Bay (西子灣), and monkeys often roared at me on the road. Mr. Zhang often walked in the woods nearby. Only Du Fa followed him. I often tried to hit a sparrow with a slingshot near where they walked. Once I hit one and showed it to Mr. Zhang. He turned to Lao Du and said, "He really hit one!" It was a backhanded compliment; I was sad to hear it.

Another memory I have from that time was when I walked by the gate of the foreigner's yard and saw an ugly dog with short legs and a long body. I told Mr. Zhang about it, and he said, "You are a country bumpkin. That is called a dachshund, and it's very expensive! The next time you see it, steal it for me."

Xueliang: "Feign ignorance." (裝糊塗).

Chapter Thirty-One

BOTH SIDES OF CHINA

In September 1948, General Fan Hanjie (范漢傑, my wife Terry's father), the commander of a Nationalist Army group of more than 150,000 soldiers, lost Jinzhou, and Chiang Kai-shek lost the Northeast. Three months later, the Nationalists lost North China. The Communist Army occupied a large area in the northeast, north China, and north of the Yangtze River.

In April 1949, the Communist Army crossed the Yangtze River and occupied Nanjing. On October 1, 1949, the People's Republic of China was proclaimed in Beijing.

Chiang Kai-shek retreated to Taiwan, taking with him only 50,000 troops.

BACK TO QINGQUAN:
END OF DECEMBER 1949 - OCTOBER 24, 1957

After Chiang Kai-shek's reinstatement in December 1949 in Taiwan, Zhang Xueliang and the group returned to Qingquan. The bad thing was that the rooms of the left-wing my family had lived in were burned down. My father could only live in the two small rooms where the original office staff lived. My mother and us kids also lived there when we went for winter and summer vacations. Mr. Zhang still lived in the four rooms on the right wing, and the fifth room was still occupied by Zhou Nianxing (周念行), who helped Mr. Zhang study the history of the Ming Dynasty.

My elder brothers came to Taiwan. At the time, my elder brother Bohan and my second brother Philip (Zhongpu) were still in high school in Chongqing. My elder brother attended the party-run Zhongzheng Middle School. He was handsome and outgoing. My second brother studied in Qinqhua Middle School. He was very smart and liked the Communists.

Before the Mainland changed colors, my father arranged for them to come to Taiwan. At first, my second brother refused. He planned to sleep in the classroom and sell ice cream for a living. But my elder brother told him they should go together. They had no money, only one white shirt on their backs. My father's colleague, Shen Zui (沈醉), the station chief of the Military Bureau, sent them on a plane to fly to Guangzhou. The stationmaster of Guangzhou was told to put them on a plane to Hong Kong, and then the stationmaster of Hong Kong sent them on a plane to Taiwan.

Finally, they came home after three years of being separated from us.

They came to Kaohsiung to see us. I was doing taijiquan (tai chi) in the yard. They stood on the bench and looked at me. I didn't meet them until I finished.

We hadn't seen each other for years, but it was as if we'd had seen each other only the day before.

We were brothers, very close in our hearts. We just didn't talk much.

Figure 31 Zhao Yidi and Bohan

When they had to go to college, they didn't have a high school graduation certificate. My elder brother learned to engrave a seal in my grandfather's home. He bought a dried bean curd and engraved a school seal of Zhong-zheng Middle School (which included high school). He

197

made two graduation certificates. Later, my elder brother was admitted to the Naval Academy; the second oldest was admitted to the Department of Philosophy, National Taiwan University, and one year later he was admitted to the Mechanical Engineering Department of Tainan Institute of Technology.

After Chiang Kai-shek retreated to Taiwan, in 1950, he summoned my father to Taipei. He asked after Zhang Xueliang's condition. Before leaving, Chiang Kai-shek wrote a note saying, "Give Comrade Liu Yiguang NT $10,000."

My father went outside. The staff outside enthusiastically asked my father whether he wanted cash or gold. My father said gold! The staff immediately gave my father three ten-ounce gold bars!

We have never had so much money! We were rich!

The saddest thing about my mother was that she couldn't feed us well over the years. Now she changed our meals to two meat dishes and one vegetable, plus fruit!

To make a long story short, the rest was taken to the Taiwan Department Store in Ximending (西門町) to earn a high interest rate. The boss, Liu Qiguang, was the mayor of Hsinchu County when we arrived in Taiwan in 1946. He was a close friend of my father, so we were sure the money would be safe there. Later, the department store went bankrupt, and we didn't get our money back. Our family was poor again.

In addition to his salary, my father was paid extra fees and special expenses for his job. No invoice reimbursement was required.

My father always gave money to my mother. My mother spent some for our food. Sometimes she spent it on fatty meats for team members who came to Taipei for business or relaxation.

Figure 32 Liu Family (undated)

But my father occasionally needed to borrow from his salary to make ends meet. The head office was very special to my father. He could borrow money and didn't have to pay it back. Therefore, my father rarely borrowed money.

199

I remember one time my mother and father quarreled because my father would not borrow more money. My mother said if he didn't, she couldn't continue managing our daily meals and she would quit her job.

And out of the blue, I cried and asked my mother to continue to take care of us.

My mother said yes, father said yes! He borrowed another two months' salary from the Bureau.

My brother Philip wrote a song for what happened: "Money is not important. You just need enough to spend. You could borrow it, and better yet we don't have to pay it back!"

My father borrowed money, borrowed cars, borrowed oil in the mainland, and borrowed salaries in Taiwan. His job had to be done, his family needed to survive.

Chapter Thirty-Two

THE SECRET AGENTS

The mountains were quiet, and the team members were young men. In the back of Mr. Zhang's love letters to Miss Four, the names of Liu Shengjun (劉生俊), Yu Ziming (禹子明), Lei Genyan (雷根彥), and Ding Changchao (丁昌潮) were mentioned. The words were sloppy; only Miss Four understood. But I also understood. Here is an explanation, plus some things Mr. Zhang did not mention.

Secret agents were also people. They lived in the mountains for eleven years and had many stories.

Liu Shengjun (劉生俊) was a member of the security team, from Henan. When he came to Qingquan in 1946, he was under thirty years old. He was very strong and dark. On the horizontal bar, he could make three complete revolutions in no time. The problem was that his Henan dialect was difficult to understand.

A beautiful girl across the river was the female owner of a Hakka grocery store. She was light skinned and only spoke Hakka. We didn't know how it started, but we often heard female singing over the river and male Henan dialogue yelling here. None of us understood what they were "crying" for. All we knew was that Liu Shengjun later reported to my father and asked permission to get married. He would go over the river to sleep at night, and he promised never to miss his duty on this side of the river. My father gave him permission to get married. When my father's team was leaving in 1957, Liu Shengjun asked to retire and stayed behind. Years later, Qingquan was a tourist attraction, with many three- or four-story buildings. How many buildings did Mr. Liu have? How many children? Did they all love singing? Love didn't need words!

Yu Ziming was transferred to Qingquan around 1955. He was tall and fat, with a big red face.

One day he was shopping in a small shop across the river and came upon an old woman of the Gaoshan tribe with a tattoo on her face. She was two heads shorter than him and struggled to look up at him several times. She came up to him and they talked a lot. The grocery store owner's translator said that she wanted her daughter to marry him. Agent Yu was scared and ran away. A few months later, Yu Ziming got married, and the bride was the daughter of the old woman.

Most of the team members were unmarried and lonely in the mountains. It was inevitable that they went to the

Zhudong Hotel to have some fun, or travelled to Taipei to alleviate their loneliness in the red light zone. Food and accommodation were available in our house, but it wasn't enough, so the Deputy always sent different team members on business trips.

In the 1950s, to encourage morale in Taiwan, President Jiang Jingguo established two basketball teams, the Seven Tigers (七虎) and Dapeng (大鵬) to represent the Army and Air Force. They played often in the military service stadium in front of the presidential palace, and the stadium was always full. I was a fan of the Seven Tigers. I watched every game by climbing in from the fence.

Later, it turned into a confrontation between the civilian fans of the Army and the Air Force, and later the Army against the Air Force.

Jiang Jingguo didn't like this, so he disbanded the two teams. The military service stadium was changed to a performance place. A Harlem basketball team, the boxer Joe Louis, an ice skating team, and others all performed there.

I was familiar with all the ways in; I knew every hole and the trees to climb to get in. I also accepted many apprentices. Later, Yuan Guangyang (沅廣洋), one of my friends who attended the Navy School, said that whenever he saw me on the tree in front, he would have the confidence to follow me.

Finally, one day, I was arrested with several of my apprentices. At the station, the police officers on duty asked each of the seven or eight students, "Which school are you from?" The answers were "Striving Hard Middle School" (強恕中學), "Success Middle School" (成功中學), "Jianguo Middle School" (建國中學), "Affiliated Middle

School of Normal University" (師大附中) and so on. When I was asked, I said, "National Taiwan University" (國立台灣大學).

The policeman officer looked at me and said politely, "Please go home."

I never climbed the fence again!

MR. ZHANG'S INTERESTS

My elder brothers came back, and we were all grown up. My youngest brother had also become a master of playing poker. Every year during the Lunar New Year, gambling was a must.

Mr. Zhang still gave us money to gamble with him and Miss Four. We also went to Qingquan in the summer, but each of us had our own obligations, and we didn't stay the entire vacation.

I don't remember what year Mr. Zhang stopped playing tennis and switched to playing Baduanjin (八段錦), a form of qigong exercise.

The tennis court was changed to a basketball court. The agents played basketball every afternoon. Philip and I always participated.

Mr. Zhang played with cameras since 1950. He used Leica cameras from Germany. As the cameras and film improved, Mr. Zhang followed the trends and bought dozens of cameras. Mr. Zhang took pictures of Miss Four, my sister Theresa, and sometimes our family and team members. My sister also took many photos.

In addition, he liked to plant flowers behind the house, collecting insects and waving nets to catch butterflies.

Figure 33 Mr. Zhang taking photo of Frank

Figure 34 Theresa, Mom, and Zhao Yidi

205

Figure 35 Mr. Zhang in the garden

Figure 36 Mr. Zhang watering plants

When I was studying in Taipei, I was their agent. I bought the "News World" and "Spring and Autumn Magazine" for Mr. Zhang. I bought "Good Housekeeping" for Miss Four. I also bought American cigarettes for Miss Four. She smoked Salems, in mint flavor. Mr. Zhang liked to read Xu Fuguan's (徐復觀) column.

When I wrote my "reports" to Mr. Zhang, I liked to add a little story. Once I wrote:

> A long time ago, I won from Mr. Zhang 40,000 yuan, and I bought a Parker pen for 10,000. The first day I tried to put ink into my expensive pen, I pushed the tip of the pen too hard to the bottom, and the tip was bent. I never got the chance to write "stupid" for myself.
>
> Sometime later, my elder brother gave me a watch, and it stopped working in a few days. My elder brother asked if I had turned the spring, and I said yes. But it turned out that every time I turned the spring, I used less force than the last time, for fear of breaking the clock.

Mr. Zhang replied to my "report." He didn't say that I was stupid. He only told me he laughed so hard that he was out of breath and said that I would be responsible if he choked!

All the letters he wrote to me were signed as "buju" (不具), no signature. It meant you know who I am and I "don't sign it." I didn't know that he was a "race hero" and "state man forever" at that time. I should have kept his handwritten letters to me. They would have been priceless documents.

Chapter Thirty-Three

BEITOU GUEST HOUSE:
MARCH 1959 - 1962

In March 1959, Zhang Xueliang moved to Beitou near Taipei and lived at Youya Road Air Force Guest House. It was the hostel of the former kamikaze death squads of Japan, the place where the suicide pilots stayed overnight. They drank there and enjoyed women.

The house was a Japanese-style bungalow, and there were many single rooms around a hall.

When Madame Chiang saw Zhang Xueliang in Xizi Bay, she asked him whether he was a Christian.

Zhang Xueliang said he was studying Buddhist scriptures.

Madame Chiang said, "You're wrong again!"

So, she sent former ambassador to the United States Dong Xianguang (董顯光) to preach to him.

In January 1960, Ambassador Dong and Madame Dong were moved to Youya Road Guest House. Ambassador

Dong was a devout Christian who taught Mr. Zhang English and explained the Bible every day.

Miss Four also joined the class, and she learned much faster than Mr. Zhang.

Dong Xianguang was full of humor and wit. He often told jokes when eating.

Diplomats were very knowledgeable about their clothes. Once we had lunch, Ambassador Dong wore suit pants and a white shirt, but pulled out his shirt in the back intentionally, indicating he was being casual.

The joke he told at that time was "replacing a leg." A man had a broken leg and found a famous doctor to help him replace his leg. It was a very successful operation. He walked like an ordinary person, except when he saw a tree, he had to walk up and spread his legs. It turned out his leg was replaced with a dog leg. Everyone laughed, and Mr. Zhang laughed the loudest.

This was the first time that Mr. Zhang had listened to someone else tell a joke, instead of being the joke teller.

Mrs. Dong was very kind and became a friend of my mother's. They moved back to their home near the end of 1960, and the two remained in communication for a long time after they left.

After Zhang Xueliang was freed from the strict control of my father, he was free to go. Whenever Mr. Zhang and Miss Four came to our house, they always took our family and other friends out to eat or sightsee.

Figure 37 l to r: Ambassador Dong, Zhang Xueliang, my mother, Miss Four, Madame Dong, Jiang Jingguo, my father (1960)

Figure 38 Family outing with Mr. Zhang and Miss Four

In June 1960, under arrangement of Madame Chiang, Dong Xianguang accompanied Zhang Xueliang to Shilin Kaige Hall for worship. That was the chapel dedicated to Chiang Kai-shek and Madame Chiang. Only special people such as Zhang Qun (張羣), the Secretary-General of the Presidential Palace, could attend.

At the end of the worship, Chiang Kai-shek and Madame Chiang would leave first. Madame Chiang nodded all the way.

At the last row where Zhang Xueliang was sitting by the aisle, she deliberately shook hands with Zhang Xueliang sitting by the aisle. This unusual behavior caught everyone's attention. That was when people found out that it was Zhang Xueliang, who had been "missing" for many years.

Figure 39 Father, Zhao Yidi, Mother, Zhang Xueliang on an outing

Zhang Qun and He Yingqin (何應欽) came to shake hands with Zhang Xueliang. Dong Xianguang introduced the pastor. This was the first time Chiang Kai-shek allowed Zhang Xueliang to make a public appearance.

After that, Wang Xinheng (王新衡), Peng Mengji, and Mo Dehui often came to the guest house to see Zhang Xueliang. After that week, Zhang Xueliang went to Kaige Hall to worship every week.

Where was Miss Four? Sorry, she had to wait four years. Madame Chiang still had arrangements to do.

How did Madame Chiang arrange for Miss Four this time? Mr. Zhang, Miss Four, my father, and mother went to Ambassador Dong's house one day. Zhang Xueliang was accompanied by Ambassador Dong to Kaige Hall to worship with Chiang Kai-shek and Madame Chiang.

Miss Four was accompanied by Mrs. Dong and my parents to worship at the church of Rongmin Hospital. Every week thereafter, my mother and sister accompanied Miss Four to worship. Eventually, she was accompanied by someone else.

In 1964, Zhang Xueliang asked to be baptized along with Miss Four. Madame Chiang told him that Christianity is monogamous, so unmarried couples could not be baptized together.

This was planned by Madame Chiang four years prior. Zhang Xueliang had to write to his wife, Yu Fengzhi, in the United States to ask for a divorce. Mrs. Zhang signed the divorce agreement. She was willing to help them. She said, "I am willing to do anything for him, including to die."

Zhang Xueliang and Miss Four finally married on July 4, 1964. Madame Chiang attended the wedding. Before the wedding, Zhang Xueliang took Miss Four to visit Madame Chiang to introduce her. Zhang Xueliang introduced Miss Four to her; this was their first meeting.

After their marriage, the new Mrs. Zhang (Miss Four) could go to Kaige Hall to worship with Zhang Xueliang.

Chapter Thirty-Four

BUILD YOUR OWN HOUSE:
1962 - 1995

In mid 1960, Jiang Jingguo suggested that Zhang Xueliang build his own house nearby. Zhang Xueliang asked Jiang Jingguo to find a place for him. Jiang found a vacant lot below the Beitou Mountain, overlooking the sea. Zhang Xueliang decided to buy it.

When the landlord Xu Bing (許丙) heard that it was Zhang Xueliang who wanted to buy, he set the price very low. Zhang Xueliang bought the 4,000 square meter lot. The land was slightly inclined from back toward the road in front. A small stream in the side yard flowed through the hillside, which was a challenge for the garden designer. I told Mr. Zhang that we could build a small dam with stones, and a wooden bridge over the dam. Mr. Zhang later raised red carp there.

Mr. Zhang wrote a check for US $30,000, withdrawn from his own account in the United States. The Security

Bureau handled it for him. A two-story bungalow with an area of about 400 square meters was chosen. The design and construction were undertaken by Lu Genji (陸根記) Construction Company (a construction company that worked with the Security Bureau to build its headquarters and the official residences and vacation homes of Chiang Kai-shek).

The house was built in early 1962 and they moved in shortly after. Jiang Jingguo sent a set of furniture as a gift.

The entrance to the downstairs led to a rectangular living room on the left and a kitchen and a dining room on the right. They were separated by a wall, and a hole was opened in the wall to allow for the delivery of food. Wu Ma had to cook and pass the dishes through the hole. I guess Miss Four had to receive the food from the opposite side.

What a difference it was from their house arrest days. A waiter would stand behind to serve the food cooked in the kitchen with a chef from one of the best restaurants of China.

I didn't know what it looked like upstairs. I only knew that the roof was a concrete platform because Mr. Zhang asked me what to do if the concrete cracked. I told him a 4 x 4 wire mesh could be added, and he could ask the contractor Lu Genji.

On the left side of the door, there were three rooms at the entrance next to the wall. Jiang Youfang lived in one room, and Gong Wengyu, the driver, lived in another.

Outside Zhang Xueliang's compound, there was a row of houses opposite the gate, where Captain Xiong Zhongqing stayed with a dozen agents. Xiong had taken over the position of my father. The duty had been changed to protection, and the funds were still paid by the Security Bureau.

Zhang Xueliang had to pay all his living expenses. He also bought a Ford car for his own use.

MISSION ACCOMPLISHED

Jiang Jingguo knew that my father was not suitable to "serve" Zhang Xueliang, so he relieved my father's duty to control him.

Figure 40 My father and mother with all his agents (1962)

The photo shows my father and all his agents taken at the end of his duty in 1962.

The photo shows Zhang Xueliang in the center, Jiang Jingguo on the right, and my father on the left. It was taken after a farewell dinner given to my father by Zhang Xueliang.

After twenty-five years together, Zhang Xueliang bid farewell to my father at Youya Road Guest House.

He told the kitchen to prepare a special dinner and took out his own preserved wine for my father. He and Miss Four invited Jiang Jingguo and Peng Mengji. With my father, the five of them ate together.

Figure 41 l to r: Liu Yiguang, Zhang Xueliang, Jiang Jingguo
(Beitou, 1962)

At the table, Zhang Xueliang told Jiang Jingguo, "Liu Yiguang is my enemy because he controlled me for twenty-five years very strictly. He is also my benefactor because he saved my life. Now he is going to leave, and I want to give him some money."

Jiang Jingguo said, "I will take care of him."

My father didn't get the money, and my mother said, "It is better this way!" My father worked honestly all his life, not to work for some money that could be counted at the end. One's value was not judged by money, because nobody could take it to the grave.

Chapter Thirty-Five

WHY ZHANG XUELIANG DIDN'T RETURN TO THE MAINLAND

After Lee Tenghui was elected president in 1990, he released Zhang Xueliang from house arrest, and he was freed to go anywhere he wished.

Zhang Xueliang and his wife (Zhao Yidi, or Miss Four) went to the United States twice in 1991 and 1993. He also expressed his willingness to go to the mainland to see if he could contribute something for the Motherland.

The Chinese Government welcomed Zhang Xueliang back to China. Deng Xiaoping (邓小平), the leader of China, asked Deng Yichao (邓颖超), wife of Zhou Enlai to write a letter to invite Zhang Xueliang to visit mainland China:

> Zhang Xueliang:
> Time never stops, it flows like water. Several decades separated by the ocean, we miss you more as time passes.
> When my husband Zhou Enlai was still alive, he always sighed deeply when thinking about you.

Now you are healthy, everything is fine, and you are interested in taking a ten thousand mile trip. We are very happy to hear this.

You have left your homeland many years, your relatives and old friends are all looking forward to seeing you.

Luckily, the wall between mainland and Taiwan gradually opened. Now the spring comes after winter, suitable for you make a trip to the mainland.

I was asked by Deng Xiaoping to invite you and Mrs. Zhang to visit mainland China at your convenience.

Come to look at your homeland, to tomb sweep, or visit relatives, or sightsee, or talk to old friends, or to permanently live here.

Here I introduce the special envoy Lü Zhengcao (呂 正操) to visit you, to explain everything.

Please tell him what you like, so that we could arrange things.

May 20, 1991

❋ ❋ ❋

On June 4, 1991, Zhang Xueliang met with Lü Zhengcao in New York. They talked for three hours. Lü Zhengcao focused on introducing him to the Communist's policy of one country, two systems, and peaceful reunification of the motherland.

Zhang Xueliang agreed with the above-mentioned claims of the Communist Party of China. He hoped that in his lifetime, he could contribute to the peaceful reunification of the motherland.

Zhang Xueliang told Lü Zhengcao, "I have done this in the past. I am willing to use my reputation to continue to work for it. Although I am over 90 years old, there is still time I could contribute. I am Chinese. I am willing to contribute to China."

After returning to Taiwan, Zhang Xueliang asked Wang Ji (王冀) to be his special envoy to go to the Mainland to discuss with relevant departments. Zhang Xueliang hoped that mainland leaders could write an invitation letter, preferably from Deng Xiaoping or Yang Shangkun (楊尚 昆), the President of the People's Republic of China.

Later, President Yang Shangkun sent a letter to President Li Tenghui inviting Zhang Xueliang to visit the mainland.

Li Tenghui asked Zhang Xueliang to the presidential palace. Li Tenghui looked very serious, holding Yang Shangkun's invitation letter, and said to Zhang Xueliang, "I have treated you very nicely. Why did you do this behind my back?"

Only then did Zhang Xueliang realize that Li Tenghui was engaged in Taiwan independence. How could he let him go to the Mainland to support reunification! Zhang Xueliang now knew that staying in Taiwan was useless. That's why he decided to emigrate to the United States. He chose Hawaii, which was not too far from China.

If Zhang Xueliang returned to the Mainland, he would surely have received the highest and warmest welcome, but he did not want that kind of vanity, because he was unable to promote Taiwan's return to China.

Zhang Xueliang's state of mind had gone to the next level. He wanted to unify China. If he couldn't do it, there was no need to return to the Mainland to receive the embrace of the Motherland.

He'd rather go to the Hawaiian beach, to taste his loneliness in a wheelchair.

Chapter Thirty-Six

AFTER THE HOUSE ARREST

In early 1962, my father left Zhang Xueliang and was transferred back to the Office of the Director of the Security Bureau as one of the three Deputy Directors. Living at home, a Jeep came to pick him up and take him to work.

It was a job my father held until his retirement. My father died at the age of 77. After I left for the United States in 1963, I only saw him alive once more in 1976, when I took my family (my wife Terry and daughters Vivian and Sylvia, then eight and six years old) to visit my parents in Taiwan.

My father only did one job in his life, taking care of Zhang Xueliang. He did his best for the party (the Guomindang) and country, and he did his best for Zhang Xueliang. He did his best for our family. His job was not a good job, but he did it as best as he could. I am proud of my father!

After my father left his job, Mr. and Mrs. Zhang still came to our house.

Their new home had a western oven, and Miss Four loved to bake pastries. She baked sweet desserts according to the recipes of "Good Housekeeping. "But Mr. Zhang didn't like sweets. Miss Four couldn't finish them herself and often gave them to my brothers and sister to help finish them.

Mr. Zhang often came to our house. He took us to Zhonghua Road to eat. Once we finished eating upstairs, we'd walk downstairs. We passed a small shop selling Shanghai crickets, and Mr. Zhang stopped to eat a bowl and asked if anyone else wanted it. Everyone shook their head. Only me, once the little fat boy, ate a bowl with him.

STUDY IN THE UNITED STATES

In March 1963, I was ready to come to the United States for graduate school. Agent Jiang Youfang took me to say goodbye to Mr. Zhang. He and Miss Four met me in the living room and gave me a New and Old Testament Bible and NT $2,000 (about $50 at the time).

Mr. Zhang told me, "You must read the Bible." Before that, Mr. Zhang also asked Jiang Youfang to take a blank plane ticket coupon and give it to me. Jiang Youfang only told me that it was from Mr. Zhang and did not explain how to use it. I was one dumb person. I didn't know that I could go to a travel agency, exchange it for a plane ticket to any place in the United States. I didn't use it and I forgot where I put it.

At that time, one needed to provide a guarantee of $2,400 for a student to study in the United States. Mine was a check borrowed from the Security Bureau. I left for the United States with slightly more than $200. I bought a freight ticket from Kaohsiung to Seattle, Washington for $150. It stopped in Japan and then arrived at the United States. It took twenty-four days of travel over the Pacific Ocean. I made my way to Los Angeles by Greyhound bus.

To save money, I lived with four men who came over to the United States on the same boat and we shared the rent. We five roommates gathered money to buy a hair clipper, and everyone cut each other's hair. Finally, when we went our separate ways, one fellow said the hair clipper belonged to him, and he took it. I still remember his face. The first thing I did when I was able to, was send the borrowed $2,400 security deposit to my father. He returned it to the Secret Service.

Chapter Thirty-Seven

ZHANG XUELIANG'S LOVES

The two great lady loves of Mr. Zhang are my tribute to end my story.

Mrs. Zhang (Yu Fengzhi)

At the age of sixteen, Zhang Xueliang married Yu Fengzhi (于鳳至), who was three years older than him. Mrs. Zhang called Zhang Xueliang "Little Master," and he called her "Elder Sister."

When "Little Master" was between sixteen and twenty years old, young and a playboy (the Chinese term was "crazy seven"), Mrs. Zhang let him play around.

Between twenty and thirty years old, Zhang Xueliang was at the top of his career, rising quickly from "Little Brigadier" to "Young Marshal." He was a hero who loved beautiful women, and beautiful women loved the hero. Zhang Xueliang kept eleven mistresses.

Mrs. Zhang couldn't control him; she was silently a good wife and mother, living in the palace and raising their daughter and three sons.

Figure 42 Zhang Xueliang and Yu Fengzhi

After Zhang Xueliang lost his freedom, Mrs. Zhang and Miss Four took turns accompanying him.

Mrs. Zhang was with him the first three years at Yuanling and Xiuwen. Those three years were the only days when Mrs. Zhang spent alone with Zhang Xueliang in their life together. The eagle had lost his wings. Zhang Xueliang would lie on his wife's lap, and she silently stroked his thick black hair. That was the only time she got to be alone with her husband, three years in their seventy-four years of marriage.

Mrs. Zhang got breast cancer in 1942, and she initially refused to go to the United States for treatment. She just wanted to stay with Mr. Zhang; one day was one more day! Mr. Zhang told her to go to the United States to cure her cancer and to mobilize public opinion to call attention to his plight. Mrs. Zhang went to the United States by herself. She didn't speak English, but managed to see a doctor, get chemotherapy, and have an operation. She got her breast cancer cured.

Later, she learned English, invested in the stock market, and after she made some money, she invested in real estate. She made a lot of money. She bought Ingrid Bergman's villa and Elizabeth Taylor's former home, both located in Hollywood. The interiors were decorated like their Beijing's headquarter, Prince Shucheng's Palace (順承王府). She lived in one with her children. The other house was left for "Little Master" and "Little Girl" (Miss Four) to live in the future when they were freed.

In 1964, Zhang Xueliang wrote to her asking for a divorce so that he could marry Miss Four. He said to her, "We will always be us!" ("我們永遠是我們!") She signed the divorce papers and said that she would sacrifice anything for him, even to die.

The divorce didn't change Mrs. Zhang. She still considered herself Mrs. Zhang for the remainder of her life. She used the name Zhang Yufengzhi (張于鳳至) on her tombstone in Los Angeles. She also left a lot for Zhang Xueliang beside her tomb.

She passed away on March 20, 1990, at 93 years old.

When Zhang Xueliang arrived in Los Angeles a year later, he looked at the empty tomb left for him, and then faced Zhang Yufengzhi's tombstone. After a long silence, he gently said, "Elder Sister, why didn't you wait for me!"

❊ ❊ ❊

Miss Four (Zhao Yidi)

Miss Four (Zhao Yidi, 趙一荻) loved Young Marshal Zhang. She went to Zhang Xueliang when she was sixteen years old. Their relationship lasted seventy-two years, until she passed away at age eighty-eight.

She spent twenty-two years with Zhang Xueliang during the house arrest days, not as a wife, but as Miss Four. She couldn't see her own son, Robert, the only son of her and Mr. Zhang. She had left him at twelve years old to live with a friend's family in the United States when she went to join Zhang Xueliang in his house arrest.

The only thing she could do was to hang a picture of her treasure on their living room wall.

The next thirty years, when Zhang Xueliang was half free, she still was Miss Four and half free until 1964 when she married Mr. Zhang. Mrs. Zhang Zhao Yidi was fifty-two years old. But she was still only half free, until 1990, when Zhang Xueliang was completely freed, and she was seventy-eight years old.

In April 1995, Zhang Xueliang and Mrs. Zhang got green cards from the U.S. Immigration and Naturalization Service. They moved to Hawaii

Figure 43 Zhao Yidi

The next five years, every Sunday, they rode wheel-chairs to church, parked on side wall, and silently prayed.

Every other day, Ling Yuanquan (林沅全)(a short and strong waiter from the later house arrest days), hired by Zhang Xueliang, pushed them on the beach.

They silently enjoyed their loneliness.

After she left (she died on June 22, 2000), Zhang Xueliang left a plot for himself near her grave in Hawaii.

Zhang Xueliang died more than one year later and used the plot he had left himself. He left the plot left by Zhang Yufengzhi in Los Angeles empty forever.

Zhang Xueliang died of illness on October 15, 2001. He had lived 100 years.

Chapter Thirty-Six

MY SIBLINGS

Each of my siblings have their own stories and memories about Zhang Xueliang. Some of my brother Philip's memories are included in this memoir, and my brother Frank's and my sister Theresa's recollections follow below. First, I will briefly provide an update of each sibling as of the writing of this memoir.

My eldest brother Liu Bohan passed away in 1992. He was the only one of my siblings who didn't leave Taiwan. He was survived by his wife and four children (three sons, one daughter), and four grandchildren. My second brother Philip Liu is a retired mechanical engineer who lives with his wife in Illinois. He was the first to leave Taiwan for the United States and has three sons (two from his first marriage), three grandchildren, and one great-grandchild. My sister Theresa Walker is a retired technical illustrator who worked at the Air Force Research Laboratories Space Vehicles Directorate and lives in Massachusetts with her husband. She has two children (a daughter and a son) and five grandchildren. My younger brother Frank Liu retired from Motorola, where he worked as an electrical engineer on multimillion-dollar base stations, and lives in Illinois with his wife. He has one daughter and two grandchildren. My youngest brother Alex Liu lives in Australia. He has four children and seven grandchildren.

The following are written by my siblings.

MY BROTHER FRANK'S MEMORIES

We lived with Mr. Zhang for many years, ever since we were very young.

From what I can remember, there was a lake in Tongzi, Guizhou, that had plenty of fish, and each of us had our own tiny fishponds. We were very excited to go catch fish every morning.

After arriving in Taiwan, we lived in Zhudong, Qingquan, until I started elementary school, and the area had hot springs with crystal clear water. I trace my love of fishing to a mountainous stream in the region and learned different methods for catching fish from the area's indigenous populations.

When I was a kid, my favorite time of the year was Chinese New Year's. Every year, Mr. Zhang would hand out red packets of money. Then we would play a card game called "70 Points." When we played pai gow, we were always very loud and lively. Mr. Zhang generously shared with us all his hard-earned knowledge about how to win at pai gow. The adults played Xiangnan card games and mahjong.

My Sister Theresa:
In Memory of Zhang Xueliang and Zhao Yidi

I will forever remember how Miss Four treated me so kindly, even better than my own mother did, and how Mr. Zhang was open-hearted, humorous, and full of laughter. The twenty-five years that we spent together will live on in my memory.

Chiang Kai-shek could not let go of the Xi'an Incident, so Zhang Xueliang lost his freedom for nearly half a century. My father became the one chosen by Chiang Kai-shek to supervise Zhang Xueliang. Our family lived with Mr. Zhang and Zhao Yidi—we lived together, we ate together, we rejoiced and suffered together—for twenty-five years.

Zhao Yidi, in those many years, lived with no freedom and with bitterness for many years. She gave me the affection of a mother and a teacher, plus a companion. This was also fate.

Mr. Zhang loved Chinese paintings, taking pictures, planting flowers, raising small animals, and could also sing Peking Opera. The details of his life, in those twenty-five years, are worth remembering and cherishing.

Here are some photos from that time.

ZHAO YIDI AND ME

Figure 44 Zhao Yidi and Theresa having afternoon tea

Figure 45 Theresa on the wood pile, Zhao Yidi sat below

Figure 46 On the wall of their living room of was a photo of Zhang Xueliang and Zhao Yidi's son Robert

Figure 47 Zhao Yidi gave Theresa makeup lessons

Figure 48 Theresa and Zhao Yidi wearing indigenous clothing

Figure 49 Zhao Yidi was a very good seamstress and made our
exercise and play clothes

Figure 50 Zhao Yidi was skilled at knitting; Theresa wearing a sweater knitted by Zhao Yidi

Figure 51 Theresa dresses up in Zhao Yidi's formal wear

241

Mr. Zhang's Art Collection

Mr. Zhang's art collection hung on the wall on his residences in Taiwan (Qingquan Hot Springs, Xizi Bay in Kaohsiung, the guest house on Youya Road in Beitou, and in his own new home in Beitou). Unfortunately, I don't know the names of all the artists in the paintings shown, except the one by Zhang Daqian (張大千), a famous artist and an old friend of Mr. Zhang.

This photo was taken in the 1950s in Zhang Xueliang's study in Kaohsiung. He had many stories to tell about his artist friends and the national and personal history behind his collection. I was impressed by the way he cherished and cared for it.

Figure 52 Theresa admiring a Zhang Daqian painting at
Zhang Xueliang's Kaohsiung study (1950s)

Figure 53 Zhao Yidi at Qingquan Hot Springs

Figure 54 Zhang Xueliang at Qingquan Hot Springs

BERNARD LIU

Mr. Zhang: A Man for All Seasons

Mr. Zhang's interests included visiting famous temples and historic sites, hiking, swimming, hunting, photography, fishing, playing mahjong and tennis. He was a man for all seasons: outdoorsman, raconteur, jokester, animal lover, and sportsman.

Figure 55 Zhang Xueliang, Liu Yiguang, and others in the mountains

Figure 56 Mr. Zhang was a man for all seasons

MY ARTWORK

In 1961, shortly before he turned 60, Mr. Zhang asked me to give my artwork to him as his birthday gift, because he knew that a lot of high-level people would come to celebrate his birthday. He knew this was a good opportunity to show off my artwork. I was moved by his support and encouragement.

Figure 57 Liu Family with Zhang Xueliang and
Zhao Yidi at his 60th birthday (1961)

In 1950, I exhibited my art in Taipei Museum's annual exhibit. This was the first important exhibit that showed my work. Zhang Xueliang was very proud of my success. Because Zhang Xueliang couldn't leave the house to attend the exhibit, he asked Mo Dehui (莫德惠), the Northeast Elder Dean of the Examination Academy to represent him

246

at the exhibit, and to recommend and praise my painting. Mo Dehui was someone people paid attention to.

Between 1946 and 1956, his Qingquan Hot Springs private retreat was his home. He lived in a 24-guest room house made of cypress wood that was Japanese-style with tatami mats. Zhang Xueliang, Zhao Yidi, Wu Ma, and Du Fa lived on the right side of the house in three rooms. Our family lived on the left side in three rooms. The rest of the rooms were for general use, including the dining room, the kitchen, the maids' quarters, and the guard's station.

In 1949, the left side of the house burned down. In 1961, a typhoon destroyed the rest of the house.

In 2000, Zhao Yidi died, and in 2001, Zhang Xueliang died. Looking back, it almost seems like a dream, but I will always have these memories and photos to remind me of these people and places, and I will always cherish these memories.

In the decades we lived together, I never heard them criticize each other. Zhang Xueliang and Zhao Yidi lived through high and low times together, always loving each other, for seventy-two years.

Figure 58 Theresa's art at Taipei Museum exhibit (1950)

EPILOGUE

This was the story of my years with Zhang Xueliang, but I will explain what happened after I left Taiwan.

When we lived with Zhang Xueliang, we were influenced by him so much. We lived so long with him that I felt like I didn't have my own personality. We heard his stories and jokes all the time. We thought about him all the time. Later, whenever I played mahjong, I would always remember him. I also remembered my mother, who loved to play mahjong.

One day, I said to myself, I have to stop thinking about him. And I did.

In my twenties, I worked in Taiwan in the Water Resources Planning Committee. My coworkers and I all dreamed of going to the United States. The jobs in Taiwan didn't pay well and weren't challenging.

In 1963, at the age of thirty, I took a cargo ship to the United States. There were twenty passengers on the ship, about fifteen of whom were students going to United States for graduate study. All we did was play poker and talk about who would get a dishwasher job. I ended up getting a job as a waiter in a Chinese restaurant in Los Angeles.

Figure 59 Author on the job in Taiwan on a suspension bridge

Our ship stopped in Japan, where I bought a Brother typewriter. We landed in Seattle, and I took a Greyhound bus, first to San Francisco and then to Los Angeles. I went with four students who were on the same boat. My junior high school classmate Li Dingmin (李定閩) helped us find an apartment where we could stay. He later found an apartment for my best friend Wang Zhaoqian and me.

Figure 60 Author as waiter in Los Angeles (1964)

I lived in Los Angeles for a year and worked as a waiter in a Chinese restaurant in Inglewood. I met my future wife, Terry Liu (Fan Tayu, 范大渝),[14] after she arrived in

---

14 . My wife is also the direct descendant of the famous Governor Lin Zexu (林則徐,1785-1850), best known for his role in instigating the First Opium War, waging a campaign against the British opium trade and dumping millions of pounds of opium into the sea. My wife's mother, Lin Jian-feng (林劍峰) was the fifth-generation daughter of Lin Zexu.

251

1964. Her father was the three-star Guomindang General Fan Hanjie (范漢傑), one of Chiang Kai-shek's confidants and favorite generals. He was the deputy commander-in-chief in Manchuria and in command of the Nationalist Army forces in Jinzhou when it fell to the Communists in October 1948. He was captured by the Communists and held in China (at a community farm for rehabilitation and later house arrest) until his death in 1976. My wife, her mother, and her siblings fled to Taiwan when the Communists took over. She left the Mainland at the age of ten and never saw her father again.

Figure 61 Author and future wife Terry (1965)

We went to graduate school at Utah State University in Logan, Utah. Terry went first. I had saved up money to go as well, but I lost the money gambling, playing poker with my roommates, so I had to stay in Los Angeles longer to make back the tuition money.

I studied civil engineering, soil mechanics, and received my master's degree in 1966. When we graduated, my first job was supposed to be with an engineering firm in New Jersey, but we only had enough money to take a Greyhound bus to Chicago. When we got there, I called Harza Engineering Company, got an interview, and was hired.

When we arrived at Chicago, it was too expensive to get two apartments for Terry and me, so a friend suggested that we get married. We did, in Wisconsin. My wife borrowed a dress from my brother Philip's wife, and I borrowed a suit from him. In Chicago, my two daughters were born, Vivian (劉沛文) in 1967 and Sylvia (劉羲文)in 1969.

Getting a job at Harza changed my life. Edelca, the Venezuelan electrical company, wanted to hire Harza engineers to go to Venezuela to help work on a large hydro-electric project. I volunteered for the job, but my boss said, "That's not a job for you," implying I was not qualified. When they couldn't find someone else who wanted to go, they sent me. Before that, Harza had sent a geologist and a department head to Venezuela. Dr. Desola, a famous geologist in Venezuela, and the geologist Harza sent got into a fight over a rock sample. When that person didn't work out, I volunteered.

We had no idea where Venezuela was and had to go to a public library to look it up. The librarian didn't know either but helped us look it up in an atlas.

We moved to Venezuela in 1976, when I was forty-two. After a month or so, my Chicago boss David Kline asked my boss in Venezuela, Gerardo Chiwali, how I was doing, and he said, "Please send another Bernie Liu." I ended up living in Venezuela for twenty-three years, until 1998, the year after Hugo Chavez attempted his first coup and things got very unstable and dangerous.

I went to Venezuela as a geotechnical engineer and ended up a hydroelectric engineer. Over the twenty-three years, we built three dams: Represa de Guri, Macagua, and Caruachi. I designed the remodel of the fourth dam, Tacoma. The combined power of the four dams is equivalent to the Three Gorges Dam in China.

I took a leap of faith going overseas to a strange country where we didn't speak a word of Spanish. That's part of my character. I was willing to venture into the unknown and succeed at it. Maybe it had to do with growing up in the unstable war years in China and taking a similar leap when I left Taiwan for the United States.

I ended up learning Spanish through work. I had a Chinese accent when speaking Spanish, and all the draftsmen laughed at me when I said, "lápiz" (pencil). Apparently, it was hilarious to them. On one of my birthdays, they gave me a giant pencil as a gag gift.

When we got to Caracas, we found an apartment through an ad in *The Daily Journal*, the English-language paper. When we met the landlord, we didn't understand enough Spanish to understand that she was renting out the apartment next to hers instead of her own. My daughters learned Spanish by playing with her daughter.

I built my entire career in Caracas. We met so many people from different parts of the world and became friends. My wife's best friends were Greek, Colombian, Lebanese, and Hungarian. Our daughters went to international and American schools and got great educations and ended up in Ivy League colleges and graduate schools. My daughter's kindergarten grade had forty-two nationalities.

My years in Venezuela were some of the best of my life. I loved going to the field in the interior of the country, where the dams were built. We would hang out with engineers and my counterpart, Zenon Prusza. After a long day of work, we would have feasts. Frank Carrera, the chief of the project, would host a party. He would give us steak as an appetizer, and for the main dish, he would serve more steak with really hot peppers. Only I could take it. We would play cards and poker and drink.

Every consultant board meeting, I made presentations. Once I was sent to Edelca management to explain. As I pointed to the charts, I said, "Este, este, este." (Spanish for "this, this, this"). At the end, two guys walked in front of me, and I asked, "¿Que the parece?" ("What did you think?"), and they said, "No entiendo chino." ("I don't understand Chinese".) But all the draftsmen and engineers in my office understood my Spanish, even if it was heavily accented.

The people in Caracas were very friendly. For parties and going anywhere, people didn't arrive on time. When we went to friends' houses, we'd show up on time but be way too early. Once, we were invited to a baptism, and the host wasn't there when we arrived; the grandmother had to pause her preparations to entertain us. When people finally arrived, we had to leave because we had to get back to our babysitter.

When we first got there, we once asked draftsmen and engineers to our house. One asked, can we bring our mother-in-law? The word spread. Everyone brought someone. We invited a bit more than ten people. More than forty people showed up in our tiny apartment. There was no place to sit; everyone took a dish and sat on the floor and ate. After they ate, they wanted to dance. We said we didn't have music. They marveled, "No dancing!"

The weather in Caracas was always great, in the 70s all year round, as it sits in a valley about 1000 kilometers above the sea level. Other great memories I have are traveling around Venezuela with my family. We would go to the beaches where I would fish, or we would sit in the shallow surf and dig for clams. We traveled to the western Andean town of Mérida and the tropical island of Margarita in the east. Once, we went with three other families (including my wife's brother, who worked in Guri for some years) on a caravan trip of four Jeeps down through the Gran Sabana (the "Great Savannah") in the south, driving to the Brazilian border. There was no road. We drove through tire tracks across the dusty plain with bandannas around our faces, with giant tepuys (flat-topped mountains) in the distance. It was so remote that we had to carry our own gasoline and water for parts of the trip, and we camped by streams.

We went back to Chicago for one last year in my career and stayed there one more year after that. I worked as a consultant for Edelca and went back to Caracas for business trips. Even though I was a year away from retirement, we left Venezuela in 1998, because we felt unsafe. A friend of ours was killed in a carjacking in a parking lot after having lunch with us at a restaurant. In another incident, one of my draftsmen was murdered. He was stabbed while he was waiting for a porpuesto (bus). My boss offered to hire a bodyguard for me, but my wife insisted that we leave.

When I retired, we moved to northern California to be

closer to Vivian and her family. They moved to Massachusetts five years later, but we stayed in the Bay Area for a total of twenty years. We moved to Virginia in 2019 to be closer to Sylvia and her family.

My life after Taiwan can be summarized in 1, 2, 3, 4, and 5. One, I married a good wife. Two, we have two good daughters. Three, I built three big dams in Venezuela. Four, I designed a fourth dam (four is also the number of mahjong players in a game; my wife and I played mahjong for many years in California with our friends). And five, I have five wonderful grandchildren: Michael, Emily, and Andrew (from Vivian and her husband John), and Sammi and Sarah (from Sylvia and her husband David).

Figure 62 front row l to r: Author, Terry, Sarah, Sammi, Emily, Michael, Andrew; back row l to r: Vivian, Sylvia, David, John (2017)

After I left Taiwan in 1963, I only saw my mother once more, when I took my family to meet my parents in 1976. We were only able to afford to go back to Taiwan after we moved to Venezuela. My mother, Long Zhizu, died at the age of seventy-two in 1981 (August 19, 1909 - November 19, 1981). I saw my father one more time at her funeral. Liu Yiguang died at the age of seventy-seven in 1982 (September 30, 1904 - July 19, 1982).

I published a version of this memoir in Chinese when I was eighty-four years old. At the writing of this English-language version, I am eighty-eight years old.

I spent twenty-five of those years with one of China's most famous political prisoners.

EDITOR'S NOTE

As the author's daughter, I worked with my father on this English version of his memoir, *House Arrest Days of Zhang Xueliang* (People's Publishing House, China, 2018). Because I don't read or write Chinese, but understand and speak it, we worked collaboratively. My dad translated his own text, and I smoothed out his English, asked him questions, and we talked through the events in the book.

We have generally used Pinyin for the romanization of Chinese words, but for a few well-known names and places, we kept the Wade-Giles system. For example, Chiang Kai-shek is the Wade-Giles name (in Pinyin, it is Jiang Jieshi), and we have used pai gow instead of paijiu. Taiwan locations, like Hsinchu and Kaohsiung are still known by their Wade-Giles names, so we kept them (instead of Xinzhu and Gaoxiong). My father's Chinese name in Pinyin is Liu Shuchi, but he has gone by Liu

Shoutze his whole life, so we kept that. We are grateful for Chinese language and Pinyin copyeditor Yilin Wang for her meticulous work copyediting the Chinese and Pinyin. Any errors or deviations from Pinyin are our doing.

In Chinese, it is common to say a person's full name, last name first. When my dad lived with Zhang Xueliang, his family always addressed him as "Mr. Zhang." In this memoir, we switched between using "Zhang Xueliang," when describing his role in history, and "Mr. Zhang," when talking about his interactions with the family. Except for the first chapter's overview of Chinese history, my father wrote the historical discussions in the memoir from his own research and memories.

In checking the dates of historical events and writing part of the historical background, I consulted the following sources:

Fenby, Jonathan. *Generalissimo: Chiang Kai-Shek and the China He Lost*. Free Press, 2005.

Shai, A. *Zhang Xueliang: The General Who Never Fought*. Palgrave Macmillan, 2014.

Spence, Jonathan D. *The Search for Modern China*. W.W. Norton Company, 2013.

—Sylvia Liu, January 2022

Made in the USA
Middletown, DE
25 November 2022

15701631R00161